Are you ready to think on your feet, speak up, stand out and get results?

[BLANK] to Brilliant!

Mastering communication skills through the power of IMPROV!

JOE HAMMER

Published by Forerunner Publishing, Scottsdale, Arizona
ISBN: 978-09968047-2-1

Bound and printed and in The United States of America

Cover design by Joe Hammer, That Small Business Guy
www.ThatSmallBusinessGuy.com
Edited by Stephanie Blain

To buy additional copies of this book, visit the author's website at www.BlankToBrilliantBook.com or www.Amazon.com Wholesale/bookstore orders available from Ingram

For more information on Joe Hammer's improv and business training services, please contact him via his official web sites:

www.YourImprovCoach.com
www.TheOutcasters.com
www.ThatSmallBusinessGuy.com

READER ADVISORY

Do Not Enter Without an Open Mind

Brutally Effective Information Follows

Consuming the information contained in **Blank to Brilliant** may cause spontaneous, highly impressive communication skills that cause positive reactions to those exposed to it.

Intentional misuse by deliberately ignoring its content may be harmful to your success.

You Are Hereby Cautioned:

- Some content may be inappropriate for people with small minds and big egos
- Your brain will begin operating faster than your mouth.
- There is a possibility of people enjoying conversations with you.
- Adverse reactions to your opinions will be greatly reduced.
- People may no longer be annoyed by your viewpoints.
- Substantial amounts of sarcasm will be eliminated.
- Opinionated comments are at risk of being eradicated.
- Others may place you on speakerphone with the confidence of a lion tamer.

This book does not include a brain.
Please use your own.

The soul permits laughter to minimize the illusion of the ego's significance.

— Joe Hammer

Dedication

Chris Farley
1964 - 1997

Chris Farley's comedic journey began at Chicago's renowned *Second City Theater,* propelling him into the spotlight as a pivotal cast member on NBC's *Saturday Night Live* from 1990 to 1995. Yet, his laughter-inducing talents didn't stop there. He embarked on a dynamic comedy film career, gracing the silver screen with his uproarious presence in iconic

movies like *Airheads, Tommy Boy, Black Sheep, Beverly Hills Ninja,* and *Almost Heroes.*

Chris Farley was more than just a comedian; he was an Improv Superstar, setting the stage ablaze with boundless energy and a fearless commitment to eliciting laughter. His zany alter ego, motivational speaker "Matt Foley," had the power to crack even his fellow cast members during sketches.

In the realm of improvisational comedy, Chris Farley stood shoulder to shoulder with the late, great Robin Williams, two luminous talents who transcended screens and stages alike, casting shadows as larger-than-life characters.

Today, we remember Chris Farley with a profound sense of loss, his absence leaving a void in the world of humor. Rest in Peace, my dear friend, for your comedic legacy lives on in the hearts of those you touched with your unbridled humor.

Growth comes when you challenge the personal opinions you have about yourself.

You can only give away to others what you have become yourself.

— Joe Hammer

Your Navigational Guide to Brilliance...

We've worked with Joe and the Outcasters team a few times now to bring their improv techniques and communication into the business corporate world. We've gotten a lot of great feedback from all of our team members, especially on the "Yes and..." concept as it's really important to better understand how to keep conversations moving - especially during really high touch meetings and presentations with our external clients. Teams always have a great time and it's also a really good opportunity to introduce team members to each other. They have a lot of fun and walk away with a lot of knowledge as well as smiles on their faces!

Lauren Mantecon, VP – Change Management, Learning and Development
JLL

Joe and his team provided a very fun and impactful experience for our executive team. I immediately saw everyone highly engaged in the art of improv and the perspective it brings to us as leaders. What a fun and valuable lesson to listen carefully before responding while having a ton of fun along the way. I would highly recommend this experience for a team!"

Lamont Yoder, CEO
Banner Baywood, Gateway and Heart Hospitals and Banner MD Anderson Cancer Center

I recently hired Joe and his team to come and teach a class of improv, especially as it relates to sales for our women entrepreneurs. When we started, our members were a little hesitant (to say the least!) and they stated, "Oh my gosh, improv. I'm not funny, I can't do this." All of their resistance and their fears came up. By the time we got to the end of the program, everybody was having an amazing time. They were laughing, they were building off one another. There was a ton of creativity and collaboration happening. They could really see how those improv skills would blend seamlessly now into their own sales process. It was an amazing session!

Vanessa Shaw, Founder & CEO
The Business Growth Academy

We had Joe at an event that we were holding for our clients and it was one of the most raved about experiences we have ever presented. They learned how to be more communicative. They learned how to take themselves less seriously. They learned how to make mistakes and just roll with it. And they learn how to get attention and be more persuasive. So, if you're looking for something that's entertaining and going to change the landscape of how you do business and how your attendees experience your event, then you want to book them. They're the best!

Suzanne Evans, CEO
Driven, Inc.

I hired Joe Hammer and his team to work with myself and a team of licensed insurance agents to help us learn to be better listeners and as a team building exercise. And within a very small window of time, Joe was able to help us move into a space of vulnerability and ease. We spend 50% of our day deciphering highly-regulated industry jargon, but the other half we get to spend with our clients and so it's important for us to understand ease of communication and how to listen more than we talk. The program genuinely increased our joy and time spent together.

Tanya Fed, Arizona Sales Market Manager
Advise Insurance

One of our spirits clients recently had a summit for a team of ambassadors in Scottsdale and we knew we were going to need to get everyone off their feet, thinking outside of the box, and really amping up their skills for telling stories and strong communication. We have a pretty outgrowing outgoing group of people as it is, but Joe really did a good job getting everyone immersed right from the get go. It was definitely one of the highlights of our summit. The improv session gave them all something to think about in terms of how they're communicating the stories about the brands they represent.

Pete Durbin, Account Director
GMR Marketing

I work in the partner sales organization in the technology field, a significant part of my job is to build trust with our partners and customers. Building trust is instrumental to the success of our organization and our partners and customer's future success. Consistently attending Joe's improv classes has played an important role in advancing my career because it teaches you the power of actively listening to understand (rather than listening to respond), allowing me to be present, and being able to pivot when a scene doesn't go as you planned in your mind. Joe is able to easily explain and provide examples of what each game is about and how it translates into real life situations. Improv has allowed me to get more comfortable with being uncomfortable because we never know which direction a scene will go, what your partner will say, or how your partner will interpret a suggestion. Whether you're wanting to become a better public speaker, getting better at dealing with adversity, or wanting to share laughs, improv will undoubtedly be useful for you. Thank you, Joe!

Kristina Sieper Wersel , Sr. Partner Sales Manager
Amazon Web Services

As a licensed mental health counselor and yoga teacher, I utilize Joe's teachings on a daily basis. Graduate programs taught me how to be a professional listener, but learning the "felt sense" is a whole other skill which includes many aspects found in Improv. Yoga teacher training programs gave me scripts and sequences, but the "yes, and..." rule helps me meet my clients and classes where they are in the present moment. Flowing with the unexpected is a life skill that helps us "tuck and roll" or "pivot and spin" when obstacles appear....and they always do! Do yourself a favor and read, learn and practice Improv with Joe. Your body and mind will be forever grateful. I know I am.

Steffany Kroeger, LAC, LMHC, E-RYT
Fit Mind Wellness

Our scholars had an opportunity to work with Joe Hammer and the Outcasters Improv Team. It was great for them to learn how they could work together and create synergy to create that awesome experience to "get it done and figure it out fast." I think it's going to be so beneficial for them in their careers as medical physicians in the future. Thank you to Joe and his team. We are so excited and looking forward to being able to utilize these skills!

Keiona Eady, PR & Communications
ElevateMeD

Joe's sessions are extra-helpful for me as a yoga instructor, because students often ask surprising questions! Unexpected things happen all the time in a room full of people stretching together, and being able to respond instead of react makes me a better instructor!

Megan Toney
Mindful Yoga and Wellness

The improv experience was very different from anything I had done before. I tend to like structure and know expectations if I am in front of a group, so standing up with no knowledge of what was to come completely put me out of my comfort zone. It required me to listen more intently and be willing to adapt to the changes that came up. I truly feel the exercise improved the way I listen and engage with my team."

Mike Herring, COO
Banner Gateway Medical Center

I walked into Joe Hammer's improv class having no idea what to expect. Having had no experience in improv I was beyond scared . I was amazed after taking that first class how it opened me up to new ideas. Improv is a way for me to grow in both my personal and professional life. The learning that I have experienced with Joe's guidance had opened me up for all new experiences. It has helped my dynamics at work and home. I'm a more comfortable and confident speaker and communicator. I'm now able to think on my feet with ease.

Kevin Kuretsky, Purser
Delta Airlines

I completely threw myself out of my comfort zone and attended improv classes. I had not done anything like that. You learn a lot of life skills by learning improv. You learn how to be really present in the moment, you learn how to communicate better, you learn how to listen, learn how to connect with other beings, and you just learn how to free yourself. Honestly, if you're considering taking an improv class, do it. The Outcasters does an incredible job. Even if you're feeling nervous or you don't know what to do, you don't have to. I have zero skills in this, but I've had so much fun and really have connected with cool friends too.

Michele Ariana
Speaker & Executive Life Coach

What a fun exercise. It really made everyone feel connected and engaged and brought a lot of energy to the room. I personally learned the power of creative thinking comes out of thinking outside of the box. I also witnessed how moving out of our comfort zones can be fun and beneficial. I tried a few of the exercises with my family and their kids that were visiting. I plan to share it again, maybe at a family reunion this Summer. Thanks for being awesome.

Derek Lythgoe, CFO
Banner Baywood Medical Center and Banner Heart Hospital

I am a team leader of a real estate team of about 13 people and I'm always doing training programs. I surprised the team and brought them to see Joe. I could tell everyone was a little nervous at the beginning, but then, as time went on, they loosened up, were making jokes and having fun. It was an awesome time. I recommend them as a team builder to bring your company or teams in to see Joe.

Dave Panozzo, CEO
The Panozzo Team

4 Joe Hammer

Foreword

Hi, I'm Vanessa Shaw, Founder and CEO of The Business Growth Academy, where we turn entrepreneurial dreams into reality. I'm a big believer in the power of improv to improve communication skills, as it teaches us how to listen actively, build on others' ideas, and think quickly on our feet. These are all essential skills for effective communication. I've witnessed this firsthand with our clients in my STELLAR program. They often struggle to find the perfect words in high-stakes situations like sales or being in front of the judge in a courtroom (many of our clients are attorneys, not criminals!). Thanks to improv, they've discovered their ability to think on their feet, which has significantly boosted their confidence.

Effective communication is essential for success in today's business world. The ability to convey ideas clearly and confidently, build relationships, and navigate challenges is crucial. As the world changes rapidly, we need to adapt our communication style to be more spontaneous, creative, and authentic.

In one of my recent client retreats, we had a room full of women entrepreneurs, consisting of attorneys, healthcare professionals, financial experts, marketers, branding agencies, and other professional service providers. Joe led them through a series of improv exercises designed to help them develop their listening skills, creativity, and confidence. They loved it!

At first, some of the them questioned how improv training could be relevant to their businesses, thinking "they had to be funny." But they quickly realized that the techniques could be applied to all aspects of communication, from networking to sales to customer service.

In *Blank to Brilliant,* Joe will teach you how to dismantle communication barriers, foster innovation, and infuse your professional interactions with a dash of the unexpected. His passion for improv and effective communication is evident in every chapter, and he inspires readers to embrace the unknown and transform it into an opportunity for brilliance.

Blank to Brilliant will transform the way you communicate. You will learn exercises that dissolve perceived barriers and techniques that transform dull moments into brilliant insights. You will have a versatile toolkit for most every conceivable interaction, from high-stakes presentations to collaborative brainstorming sessions to impromptu elevator pitches. Joe's wisdom will infuse your communications with a fresh breath of authenticity.

His insights and expertise explore the intersection of structured strategy and candid imagination. He demonstrates how the principles of improv can launch a profound shift in how we engage with colleagues, clients and audiences, as well as the challenges they often bring.

Blank to Brilliant is a must-read for anyone who wants to improve their communication skills. It is especially relevant for business professionals, but it can also be beneficial for students, teachers, and anyone else who wants to learn how to communicate more effectively.

It's time to step beyond the boundaries of conventional communication and chart a course towards brilliance! Unleash your "inner improviser" and embark on a journey that promises to enhance your business acumen and awaken your creative spirit.

Your communication transformation begins here!

Vanessa Shaw
Founder & CEO
The Business Growth Academy
Scottsdale, Arizona

The improv muscle, once exercised and toned, will assist you in taking fast, bold and decisive actions in your life.

— Joe Hammer

From the Author

In our fast-paced and dynamic world, we are constantly bombarded with information, leading to what can be described as "information overload." This can hinder effective communication, which has become more crucial than ever, as it lies at the core of all human interactions.

Following the successful launch of my book, *The Improv Edge: How the art of improv can boost your confidence, enrich your life and fast-track you to a more energized and motivated presence!*, I now find myself back at the keyboard, assembling another valuable resource. This one focusing on the value of improv in effective communication within the business world.

Since the release of *The Improv Edge,* I have hosted numerous *Influential Interactions* workshops for forward-thinking companies. Throughout these sessions, I have continuously fine-tuned the principles and concepts to better align with the specific needs of companies that understand the significance of incorporating improv into their communication strategies.

Allow me to introduce you to *Blank to Brilliant: Mastering Communication Skills Through the Power of Improv!* This book explores how principles of improv can enhance communication and connections with others, stimulate creativity and innovation, foster trust, and provide inventive problem-solving techniques.

These skills are essential in the ever-evolving and unpredictable business environment.

Drawing from years of study and teaching improv, I can attest that this art form goes beyond mere laughter. By incorporating improv techniques, you will improve communication in all aspects of your life.

When you effectively utilize improv in your communication efforts, you are essentially conveying trust and belief in your colleagues' valuable contributions. By embracing the "Yes, and..." mindset central to improv, you will build trust, rapport, and foster a more innovative work environment.

Blank to Brilliant offers something for everyone, whether you are a business professional, student, or simply seeking to enhance your communication skills. It will transform your perception of communication and serve as an essential resource to unlock your full communication potential.

I invite you to embark on this journey of discovery and growth with me. Together, we'll unlock your potential and unleash your inner improviser! I hope you derive as much enjoyment from reading this book as I did from writing it.

Now, let's dive in and get to work! Please drop me an email and let me know how you're doing. I love to hear success stories!

Enjoy!

Joe Hammer
May 23rd, 2023 | Scottsdale, Arizona
YourImprovCoach.com | Joe@YourImprovCoach.com

Are you ready to think on your feet, speak up, stand out and get results?

[BLANK]
to
Brilliant!

Mastering communication skills through the power of
IMPROV!

JOE HAMMER

Be a "YES!" in a world full
of "NOs."

— Joe Hammer

Introduction

Are you searching for effective techniques to enhance communication, collaboration, and creativity in your company?

Look no further than improv!

Traditional communication training and techniques often fall short, leaving employees uninspired and disconnected. However, improv offers a powerful solution to transform business communication by fostering creativity, building trust, and cultivating a positive and productive work environment. It is an essential skill for success in the modern workplace.

By embracing the principles of improv, you will unlock higher levels of innovative communication, teamwork, and leadership. You will learn to think on your feet, adapt to unexpected situations, and be present in the moment. Improv encourages you to confront your fears and become comfortable with uncertainty.

You may perceive improv as a daunting task, believing it to be beyond your capabilities. However, in reality, improv is a fundamental aspect of our daily lives. Think about everyday conversations with friends. Do you plan the exact words you will say beforehand? Certainly not! You improvise! While improv can be intimidating, it is also incredibly rewarding. Engaging in this distinctive art form offers valuable lessons, including the development of a playful mindset, active listening, collaborative spirit, and enhanced creativity. These skills lie at the core of everybody!

Improv is a gateway to unlocking your communication potential and reaping the benefits of an engaged and dynamic workforce. Embrace the lessons and experiences that improv offers, and witness the positive impact it can have on your business and personal growth.

Whether you're on stage giving a presentation, managing staff, or working with a development team, the tools of improvisation can be invaluable in your everyday life. These powerful instruments allow you to create relationships, environments, situations, and conflicts without the constraint of a script.

In *Blank to Brilliant*, I draw on my extensive experience studying, teaching and using improv principles, providing engaging techniques, practical exercises, and real-life examples. My goal is to transform your approach to communication and equip you with the tools to unleash your full potential!

To truly grasp the fundamentals of improv, you must recognize the value of spontaneity in your daily interactions. We often fall into routine patterns, greeting people the same way, taking the same routes, and responding with the same answers. Improv challenges us to step out of our comfort zones, break free from familiar patterns, and react differently.

Throughout *Blank to Brilliant,* you'll discover practical insights and exercises to improve communication skills, build stronger relationships, and foster a collaborative and creative work environment. By embracing an "improv mindset," you will demonstrate trust and value for your colleagues, leading to a more innovative and collaborative work environment.

You will notice that some topics overlap between chapters. These repetitions serve a purpose. They highlight essential aspects of effective business communication that deserve emphasis. Consider them like an extra topping on a pizza; they enhance the flavor!

Now let's get to work, shall we?...

Join Joe for a live improv class in Scottsdale, Arizona!

The destination is important, but it's most often the detours that make the trip worthwhile.

— Joe Hammer

Chapter 1

What is Improv?

Improv, short for "improvisation," is a form of theater or comedy in which most or all of what is performed is created spontaneously by the performers. Unlike scripted performances, improvisers create characters, stories, and dialogue in the moment, without prior planning or rehearsal.

Improv is the wonderful art of creating something out of nothing.

Wikipedia describes it as *"the activity of making or doing something not planned beforehand, using whatever can be found. Improvisation in the performing arts is a very spontaneous performance without specific or scripted preparation. The skills of improvisation can apply to many different faculties, across all artistic, scientific, physical, cognitive, academic, and non-academic disciplines."*

It further states, *"Improvisation also exists outside the arts. Improvisation in engineering is to solve a problem with the tools and materials immediately at hand."*

Where It All Started

Theatrical improvisation, as we know it today became mainstream in the 20th century, mainly through the efforts of

theater academics, acting coach and
educator Viola Spolin (1906-1994).
Spolin developed a series of games
and exercises to help actors improve
their improvisational skills, become
more present in the moment, more
aware of their surroundings, and
more responsive to their fellow performers. Spolin's approach was

Viola Spolin

based on the idea that improvisation was not a talent, but rather a skill that could be learned through practice and training. She focused on developing skills like listening, observation,
and spontaneity, which are essential for successful improvisation.

Spolin, along with her son, *Paul Sills,* and other influential
figures such as *Del Close, Joan Littlewood, Clive Barker,*
Keith Johnstone, Jerzy Grotowski, and *Augusto Boal,* developed a series of games and exercises aimed at helping actors
enhance their improvisational skills. The focus was on becoming more present in the moment, heightening awareness of
surroundings, and becoming more responsive to fellow performers.

These improvisational games were frequently employed as
warm-up exercises for actors before rehearsals or performances, and they also played a role in the development of improvisational theater. Additionally, they served as a creative
method to rehearse dramatic material, helping actors overcome anxiety by simulating challenging scenes that might in-
duce fear in real life.

Paul Sills played a significant role in popularizing improvisational theater. He founded the *Compass Players,* which eventually led to the establishment of the *Second City Theater* in Chicago, making it the first improvisational theater company in the United States.

Paul Sills

Drawing from his mother's techniques, Paul trained and directed the company, focusing on creating satirical improvisational theater that addressed current social and political issues. He conducted workshops for Second City actors and the general public, contributing to the widespread adoption of improvisational theater as a comedy form known as "Improv."

The opening of the Second City Theater in December 1959 marked a pivotal moment, as it became one of the most influential comedy theaters globally. Numerous actors, writers, and directors emerged from Second City, having gained formative experiences and training there. Notable alumni include *Bill Murray, Gilda Radner, John Candy, John Belushi, Dan Aykroyd, Del Close, Eugene Levy, Mike Myers, Steve Carell, Tina Fey, Amy Poehler,* and many others.

Improv was not commonly seen on television until the arrival of *Robin Williams,* a master improviser, in the popular sitcom, *Mork & Mindy.* Williams was given specific sections in each episode to freely showcase his highly developed comedic improv skills.

Since then, improv theaters have proliferated worldwide, offering improvisation comedy training to people from all walks of life. Shows like, *Thank God You're Here, Kwik Witz,* and *Whose Line Is It Anyway?* significantly boosted the popularity of improv comedy on television worldwide. Personalities like *Drew Carey, Ryan Stiles, Colin Mochrie, Brad Sherwood,* and *Wayne Brady* became synonymous with hilarious televised improv games.

Contemporary improv troupes continue to showcase their talents globally, often performing in small theaters and comedy clubs. They engage in impromptu scenes based on ideas and suggestions from the audience, continually refining their skills in emotional responsiveness to imaginative situations through regular improv training.

AS HUMAN BEINGS, WE POSSESS A NATURAL INCLINATION FOR IMPROVISATION.

To improvise is to expand and heighten the discoveries in the moment. As human beings, we possess a natural inclination for improvisation. We engage in improvisation in our everyday lives, constantly adapting to challenges with the tools available to us at that moment. Whether it's putting together a last-minute dinner, organizing a birthday party, or repairing a broken vase, we improvise! How many times have we used a knife edge or a key as a makeshift screwdriver? And let's not forget the invaluable contributions of Duct Tape and Super Glue, which often save us from the misfortune of being unable to improvise a fix for a broken item.

It's No Longer Just for the Stage!

In recent years, improv has gained recognition beyond its traditional association with comedy and entertainment. It is now widely embraced as a valuable tool by companies aiming to enhance their staff's communication skills and cultivate a more collaborative and creative work environment.

I have observed that students who have immersed in improv training experience a greater sense of ease in their personal lives and professional careers. They find more enjoyment in their daily experiences and approach disappointments and setbacks as opportunities for growth. Similar to their improvisation work on stage, they embrace unexpected situations as gifts and respond to them positively, seeking a creative resolution!

Life Has No Script

Life is not predetermined. There is no set path that we are all meant to follow. Instead, we are all free to create our own unique journey in life. This can be both daunting as well as liberating. It can be daunting because it means that we are responsible for our own choices and our own destiny. It can be liberating because it means that we have the power to create the life that we want. Improv assists in the liberation process!

There are many benefits to embracing the life "without a script." When we stop trying to live up to another's expectations, we can begin to live our own lives. We can make choices that are true to ourselves, even if they're not what others think we should do. We can also be more open to new experiences and opportunities. When we are not bound by a script, we can be more spontaneous and creative... so bring on the improv!

Sure, it can sometimes be scary to let go of control and face the unknown. It can also be difficult to deal with setbacks and disappointments. However, the rewards of living a more fulfilling life are worth the challenges. When we live our lives on our own terms, we are happier and more satisfied.

Improv allows us to be present in the moment; simply paying attention to what is happening "right now" and not worrying about the past or the future. It also allows the freedom of being open to change. Change is inevitable, so why not embrace it? When we resist change, we create unnecessary stress and anxiety. Instead, we must embrace change as an opportunity for growth and learning.

As in an improv scene, life too can be full of surprises. We must be flexible. When we are flexible, we are better able to adapt to change and to overcome challenges. With flexibility comes creativity and confidence, two important abilities that will assist us in finding new solutions to problems and creating new opportunities. Confidence allows us to take risks and step outside of our comfort zone.

A study by researchers at the *University of Michigan* and *Stony Brook University* found that just 20 minutes of improv can increase feelings of comfort and tolerance for uncertainty. The study, which was published in the journal *Thinking Skills and Creativity*, involved 100 participants who were randomly assigned to either an improv group or a control group. The improv group participated in a 20-minute improv workshop, while the control group did not participate in any improv activities.

After the workshop, the participants in the improv group reported feeling more comfortable and tolerant of uncertainty than the participants in the control group. They also reported feeling happier and more creative. The researchers believe that improv helps people to develop a number of skills that are important for dealing with uncertainty. These included:

Active listening: Improv requires participants to listen actively to their fellow improvisers in order to build on what they have said. This helps people to develop the ability to focus on the present moment and to be open to new ideas.

Acceptance: Improv requires participants to accept the unexpected and to "roll with the punches." This helps people to develop the ability to cope with change and to be more flexible in their thinking.

Collaboration: Improv is a collaborative activity, and it requires participants to work together to create something new. This helps people to develop the ability to build relationships and to work effectively as a team.

The researchers believe that the findings of their study have important implications for both individuals and organizations. For individuals, improv can be a valuable tool for developing the skills they need to deal with uncertainty in their personal and professional lives. For organizations, improv can be used to improve communication, collaboration, and creativity.

Additionally, improv experience has been shown to promote divergent thinking, uncertainty tolerance, affective well-being, and social interaction. Its principles have been used by therapists to help clients with a variety of mental challenges, including anxiety, academic performance, and general well-being. I have personally used improv principles in my clinical hypnotherapy practice to help clients become more spontaneous and responsive to their needs.

Throw away life's scripts. If you're not living on the edge, you're taking up too much space!

The Improv State of Mind

Spontaneity. Confidence. Creativity. Trust. Acceptance. Commitment. Listening. Character. Support. Teamwork.

Do any of these sound like traits you may like to put to work in your life, relationship or career? Then you must say YES to "The Improv State of Mind!"

Improv doesn't rely on pristine acting skills or how "naturally funny" you may be. Improvisation really isn't even about comedy; it's about actively listening, reacting, and being focused – all while being present in the moment at a very high level. In a performance setting, it means listening to what a fellow player says, accepting what was said without rejection, then building upon it. In business communications, it means *accepting any and all ideas brought to the table, then adding supporting information to those ideas.*

Using techniques and rules of improv, you can refine your communication skills and enjoy a more jubilant version of yourself to your family, career and daily routines. You will have the ability to quickly "think on your feet," react and briskly adapt to unexpected events and circumstances you didn't plan for!

As humans, we are social creatures, and improv inspires us to truthfully see, hear and value others, all of which strengthens relationships while encouraging risk-taking and innovation. Whether selling your idea to a loved one, supervisor, co-worker or audience members during a presentation, improv training will enhance your skills.

After reading and implementing the principles I've outlined in *Blank to Brilliant,* you will soon be living in the "Improv State of Mind!"

Our Brains During Improv

Improv thinking is akin to that of "flow state." In his book, *Flow: The Psychology of Optimal Experience*, author Dr. Mihaly Csikszentmihalyi describes flow as *"the optimal psychological state when one is engrossed in activity."* He indicates that during flow states, time can be distorted, and individuals can lose their reflective self-consciousness.

We often refer to this as being "in the zone." This is the playground of improvisers when they put their inhibitions and self-doubt aside and boldly focus on their fellow players and the scene at hand.

Through active listening and focused attention, improv training strengthens our capacity to cope with uncertainty, manage anxiety and boost our creative thinking. Being open to our fellow players requires a nose-to-the-grindstone effort, risk and engagement. This makes us more adaptable to piloting the increasingly complicated world we live in.

Improv is actually a creative experience that nourishes our brains! A 2017 study published in the *Journal of Mental Health* looked at improv as a therapeutic intervention. It found meaningful improvement in symptoms of anxiety, depression, and reduction of perfectionism (which is a significant source of stress). That's great news, right? The study was conducted by researchers at the *University of California,* San

Diego, involved 32 participants who were randomly assigned to either an improv group or a control group. The improv group participated in a 12-week improv workshop, while the control group did not participate in any improv activities. After the workshop, the participants in the improv group reported significant improvements in their anxiety and depression symptoms, as well as their self-esteem, social skills, and overall well-being. The researchers found that improv can be an effective therapeutic intervention for people with anxiety and depression because it:

Helps people to develop a growth mindset: Improv requires participants to be willing to take risks and to make mistakes. This can help people to develop a growth mindset, which is the belief that their abilities can be developed through effort and practice.

Helps people to build resilience: Improv requires participants to deal with the unexpected and to bounce back from setbacks. This can help people to build resilience, which is the ability to cope with stress and adversity.

Helps people to connect with others: Improv is a collaborative activity, and it requires participants to work together to create something new. This can help people to connect with others and to build relationships.

Couple all this with the laughter and social bonding produced by improv's imaginative interaction, and we have the foundation for a creative, socially rewarding experience. We'll enjoy the benefits of positive behavior therapy without the discomfort and costs of a shrink!

Improv creates "just enough" discomfort to trigger our minds to react outside of our conventional left-brain analytical processes. As a result, we are blessed with strength and greater adaptability when faced with a stressful life event or situation. Further, we discover better receptivity to ideas from others.

The practice of improv also delivers a blissful quartet of neurotransmitters molecules responsible for your happiness and delight. They are *Endorphin, Dopamine, Serotonin* and *Oxytocin.* In our everyday life, it's often a challenge in getting these critters released into our system; however, improv principles will come to the rescue and assist putting them to work for you!

Another area of the brain affected by improv practices is the *Default Mode Network* (DMN). It's best known for being active when a person is not focused on the outside world. During DMN, the brain is at a wakeful rest -- such as that during daydreaming, mind-wandering, when we are thinking about others, thinking about ourselves, remembering the past or planning for the future.

During the practice of improv, there is strong evidence that DMN is deactivated. This is because we become more involved in discovering the exterior world and less involved with managing our inner world... that is, our judgement, self-awareness and preoccupation with other things.

Rick Hansen of *UC-Berkeley's Greater Good Center* says, "... Neurons that fire together, wire together. Mental states become neural traits. Day after day, your mind is building your brain."

Heavy stuff, but totally in alignment with the power of improv's ability to assist us in truly "changing" our minds!

And here's the best part...

Studies have shown that improv shuts down the part of the brain involved in self-censoring! It does so by activating the part of the brain involved in creativity. When we improvise, we are required to think on our feet and come up with new ideas. This requires us to tap into our creative side and to let go of our inhibitions!

When we improvise, we experience decreased activity in the dorsolateral prefrontal cortex (DLPFC). This is a region of the brain that is involved in self-censorship, planning, and decision-making. This decreased activity allows us to let go of our inhibitions and to focus on the creative process!

See, our brains actually love the Improv State of Mind!

Just Relax...

The thoughts of standing in front of a group and improvising dialog often provokes thoughts of stage fright and fear of the unknown. The seasoned improvisor, however, sees the potential of opportunities and adventures into that unknown. They see a chance to engage with others, play and make stuff up!

The greatest scenes emerge when two people allow themselves to be vulnerable.

My experience teaching improv has demonstrated that people of all ages and backgrounds have chosen to become motivated, to step out of the box of life's predictability and embrace the thought of spontaneous conversation... creating something out of nothing! However, many of us have become accustomed to surveying a scene, situation or circumstance, and observe as much information as possible before taking action. This is the case with the classic "over-thinker."

This social anxiety many times holds us back from reaching our full potential. We are afraid of what others may think. With improv, you don't have the time to get stuck in your head; you have to keep the scene moving. If you wait for the "perfect" thing to say at the "perfect" time, nothing will ever happen.

The improv muscle, once exercised and toned, will assist you in taking fast, bold and decisive actions in your life.

The best way to change almost anything in life is to continually lean into it. Train yourself to relax through exposure to whatever it is that's perceived to be the challenge. In doing so, you release your imagination to do its job.

Relax, little grasshopper. Just relax.

Brain-Boosting Benefits of Improv!

From one of my students...

I have been taking improv classes for nine months with Joe Hammer. I have had multiple sclerosis for 26 years, and it has affected my cognitive and memory skills.

*Two weeks ago, I was retested for cognitive issues by my neurologist, Dr. Blake. I was absolutely shocked and relieved by the results. My depression had gone from **severe** to **mild** without medication. My cognitive problem-solving and memory issues had improved from **average** to **superior**.*

Dr. Blake and I agreed that the brain work from improv had helped me immensely, and she advised me to keep doing it. "I can do that," I said, "The only side effect is laughter!"

Thank you, Joe, for your time and patience. Please know that you are making a difference in people's lives. I am so grateful.

— Paula McIntyre

Also see: **Psychology Today** - *New Research Highlights the Brain-Boosting Benefits of Improv:* https://tinyurl.com/blanktobrilliant

The results you experience in life are forged from the choices you've made.

If you desire better results, make better choices.

— Joe Hammer

Chapter 2

Improv Insights

Okay, enough background into the many benefits of improv in our lives. Let's explore how improv principles can be applied to enhance your business communications and achieve greater success. Whether you're a seasoned business professional, entrepreneur or eager team member, the insights we'll discuss will help you develop the mindset and skills necessary to communicate more effectively, collaborate more seamlessly, and generate innovative ideas.

There are several reasons why improv is highly relevant to business communication. Improv encourages *active listening*. Improvisers must actively listen to their fellow players to create a cohesive and entertaining performance. Similarly, in business, active listening is crucial for effective communication. When we listen actively, we can understand our colleagues' perspectives and respond to their ideas and concerns.

Secondly, improv promotes *collaboration*. Improvisation requires performers to create a scene or story. This same principle applies in business, where successful companies rely on their employees to work together towards a common goal. By participating in improv exercises, staffers can learn to trust their colleagues, work more effectively as a team, and ultimately, create more innovative and creative solutions.

Thirdly, improv teaches players to *embrace uncertainty and take risks*. In the business world, change is constant, and unexpected challenges can arise at any time. Improv will assist in developing the confidence to adapt to these changes and tackle them with creativity and flexibility. By embracing uncertainty and taking risks in a safe and supportive environment, you can become more resilient and better equipped to handle the challenges of today's hectic business environment.

Fourthly, improv will *improve your public speaking skills*. Improvisers must be able to think on their feet, respond quickly to unexpected situations, and engage with their audience. These skills are essential for effectively presenting information in the business world. You will be more confident when speaking in front of others, and deliver more engaging and impactful presentations.

Finally, improv promotes *active kindness* as it is built on acceptance, respect, and support. These principles create a safe and supportive environment where individuals can take risks and make mistakes without fear of judgement. By practicing active kindness in the workplace, staff members create a more positive and productive work environment where everyone feels valued and supported.

Mindfulness

Jon Kabat-Zinn, a leader in the field, defines mindfulness as *"paying attention in a particular way; on purpose, in the present moment and non-judgmentally."*

That's IMPROV!

The policies of mindfulness are fully aligned with the fascinating world of improv. Both mindfulness and improv are incredibly powerful tools ready to be put to work in today's demanding business world. They allow us to accept and embrace an emotion or situation - without the desire to control it.

Being mindful is something we improvisers are trained to do. And the best part? Through their laughter and applause, our audiences actually reward us for it!

Mindfulness positively affects our career, communications, relationships and life in general. By aiming to be in the present, rather than thinking about all of the other things in our head, we are better listeners. We can respond more authentically in the moment. We are relaxed under pressure and confident in our direction!

Mindfulness is often referenced as "quieting the mind." We've all heard that we should "leave our troubles behind," right? If the day's stresses and challenges are stuck in your mind, you are distracted from focus and not present with the task at hand.

As improvisers, we have to pay astute attention to what is going on with our scene partners at all times. It is only through focus and awareness that we can understand what's happening in our scenes. Only then we are able to add supporting information and support our fellow performers in the scene. Improvisers are active listeners who not only *hear* our fellow players but *observe* them as well.

We must be present. If we are thinking about what happened five minutes earlier or what direction the scene should take in the future, we are no longer in the present moment. These same processes hold true when conducting business with a prospect, client or team member.

Through improv, you will become a master of mindfulness. You will slow down those burdensome, random thoughts that take up precious space in your brain. Improv will quickly have you seeing how magnificent present moments really are!

Validation

Everyone wants validation; it's a common desire in humanity. *We all want to know that we matter and what we say is heard.* Whether on stage, in the boardroom or having a conversation with a friend or loved one, we must always be fully present.

How many times have you been in a conversation with someone only to discover their mind to obviously be in another place? Unfortunately, passive listening is all the rage today. People just nod their heads while eagerly awaiting their turn to speak.

If I start a scene by saying, *"Hey Mike, I had a flat tire this morning,"* and he responds with, *"I was thinking maybe we should go to the casino later,"* he was not only failing to listen but obviously had an alternative plan as to where he desired the scene to go. How many times has this type of *"WTH?"* response happened in your conversations?

Acknowledge other's feelings. Now this doesn't necessarily mean that you have to agree with them, but it does mean that you must let them know that you understand how they are feeling. For example, if your coworker is telling you about a stressful project they are working on, you might say something like, *"I understand that you're feeling overwhelmed."* Reflect back what they have said in your own words. This demonstrates that you've been listening and are trying to understand their point of view.

I'll go into more detail on Mindfulness and Validation techniques in upcoming chapters, but I want to plant the seed of their importance in effective communication now.

That Damn Inner Critic

Our inner critic is that irritating little voice in our head that routinely attempts to sway us away from anything outside our comfort zone. This negative and often debilitating private dialog we have with ourselves causes us unnecessary and unwanted grief.

We've all heard it rattle off hindering statements in an attempt to knock us down...

"I can't do this."

"I'm going to sound stupid."

"Nobody is going to like this."

"I'll never get a laugh."

Those statements are just as bad as going into a job interview with the mind chatter asserting, *"I'll never get this job."* You cannot present confidence when this sarcastic and corrosive devil is on your shoulder!

These negative Jedi mind tricks can quickly turn into self-fulfilling prophecies, but only if we allow them to do so. You must avoid allowing this destructive and fear-inducing dialog to get into your head. Fear is nothing more than *misplaced attention*. It's a natural human emotion that's designed to

FEAR IS NOTHING MORE THAN MISPLACED ATTENTION.

protect us from harm. This means that we are often afraid of things that aren't truly dangerous! This can lead to anxiety, stress, and other negative emotions.

There are a few reasons why fear can be misplaced. One is that *our brains are wired to focus on the negative.* This is because our ancestors paid more attention to potential threats. As a result, we are naturally more likely to be afraid of things that are new, unfamiliar, or that we do not understand.

The second reason why fear can be misplaced is that *we have learned to be afraid of things through our experiences.* If we have a negative experience with something, we many times develop a fear of it. For example, if we were bitten by a dog as a child, we could develop a fear of all dogs.

Finally, fear can also be misplaced if we are *constantly bombarded with negative messages*. If we are continually hearing about crime, violence, and other dangers, it is natural to start to feel afraid. Turn off the mockingbird media newscasts. You don't need them.

The good news is that fear is not permanent. It is possible to overcome misplaced fear by changing the way we think about and react to it, and improv will do so by challenging your thoughts, focusing on the positive, and taking small steps towards facing and overcoming your fears.

Your inner dialogue will either power your success or prevent you from reaching your full potential. Our thoughts, whether real or imagined, significantly influence how we feel and behave. When added to our historic negative thought patterns, caustic self-talk will covertly lead us on a path to self-destruction.

If you are overly critical of yourself, you're not alone. Most people experience the inner critic's continual attempts at nurturing self-doubt and negative self-reflections. Whether on stage, applying for a job, in a team meeting or addressing an audience during a presentation, you must practice taming your inner critic. You don't have to be a victim of your own verbal maltreatment!

The inner critic thrives on perceived fears and we must focus on redirecting it. Here are some proven techniques to not only tackle negative thoughts, but replace them with more constructive dialog with yourself...

Release focus on the outcome. Many of us are finding ourselves strangled by what I call "the planning instinct." This is many times the hardest part for some people to let go of. When undertaking a project, we naturally have the result we desire in our minds. We want our party to go without a hitch. We want our new photos to look the best, the meeting to start on time, or the Hawaiian vacation to be perfect. However, the problem is *that the more particular we are of the final result we expect, the more likely we are to be disappointed.* In life, just as in improv, things seldom turn out exactly as planned. Let go of outcomes.

Develop a conscious awareness of your thoughts. Unfortunately, we are used to hearing (and sometimes *believing*) our own often negative self-narrations. In doing so, we have become unaware of the subconscious messages we're sending ourselves. Be conscious of what you're thinking about. Become cognizant of the fact that just because you "think" something doesn't necessarily mean it's true. Our thoughts are many times exaggerated, subjective, and inconsistent with our real-world, real-life sense of being.

Challenge the thought. Thoughts are just thoughts, nothing more, nothing less. Experts estimate that our minds think between 60,000 to 80,000 thoughts a day. That's an average of 2,500 to 3,300 thoughts per hour! When you find yourself obsessing about a negative thought, ask yourself if the thought is meaningful, valid or necessary.

Change the thought. For visual folks like me (we tend to think in pictures), consider mentally changing the picture. Distort the negative picture. If it's in color, make it black and white. If it's big, make it small. If it's a "booming voice" in your mind, reduce it to a squeaky, less desirable and funny voice. These are common practices in Neuro Linguistic Programming (NLP).

Stop reflecting and replaying. When you do happen to make a mistake or experience a bad day, don't replay the events over and over in your head. This only exacerbates the negative thought process. When you find yourself reflecting and replaying, avoid telling yourself, "not to think about it." Like the time-worn adage, "don't think of a pink elephant," the more you try to avoid *thinking* about something, the more you're likely to *focus* on it.

In psychology, this phenomenon is known as the *ironic process theory,* first proposed by Daniel M. Wegner in 1987. The theory suggests that when people try to suppress a thought or an emotion, they actually increase the likelihood of thinking about it or feeling it. Wegner's research found that when people were asked not to think about a white bear, they actually thought about it more often than people who were not given any instructions. This led Wegner to conclude that trying to suppress a thought actually makes it more likely to come to mind. When we try to suppress a thought, we actually focus our attention on it. This can make it more difficult to get the thought out of our minds.

Accept your thoughts and feelings. The first step is to accept that you are having the thought or feeling. Trying to suppress it will only make it worse. Instead, distract yourself with an activity. Go for a walk, organize your desk, or start talking about a different subject. In doing so, you will halt self -debilitating thoughts before they spiral out of control.

Ask yourself what advice you'd give to a friend. If your best friend expressed their own feelings of self-doubt to you, you would never tell them that they can't do anything right, they're stupid, or they don't know what they're talking about, right? Of course not. You would offer them compassionate words of encouragement and advise them things are not as they see them. Knowing this, why are we so quick to say undesirable things to ourselves? Treat yourself with the kindness you'd demonstrate to your friend. Provide words of encouragement to yourself!

Examine the evidence. Recognize when your thoughts are melodramatically negative. Examine the evidence that both supports as well as refute those thoughts.

If these adverse thoughts tend to continually resurface, draw a line down the middle of a legal pad. On the left side, list all the evidence that supports the negative thought. On the right side, write down all the evidence that refutes the negative thought. Now study the real evidence on both sides of the argument. In doing so, you can observe the situation with more rationality and with less emotion.

Consider the actual outcome if your thoughts were valid. We often imagine a small situation escalating into a major catastrophe, but in reality, that rarely happens. The worst-case scenario is usually not as terrible as our anxious minds project. For instance, if you anticipate feeling embarrassed when sharing your ideas in a team meeting or sales presentation, ask yourself, *"How bad would it truly be?"* Even if you do feel embarrassed, could you recover from it, or do you believe it would disastrously end your career or life? Always remind yourself that you have the capability to handle problems, and they rarely lead to catastrophic consequences.

Balance. There's a substantial difference between telling yourself you're not good enough and reminding yourself you can always work to become better. Accept your flaws and areas needing to be addressed; give attention to areas you desire to be better in. Accepting your weaknesses for what they are doesn't mean they have to stay that way. Acknowledge that you, like all human beings, have flaws; just be determined to remain a "work in progress" as you strive to become better!

Once you begin converting pessimistic thoughts into more rational and credible statements, your disrespectful inner critic will take a much-needed vacation. You'll soon be more attentive and flowing in the moment!

Never Failures, Just Revelations!

In improv, as in life, failures are necessary to learn. No matter how hard we try, failures will always be a part of our lives. The discovery of new ideas and directions are actually the results of the failing process and a necessity in our process of growth. Our thoughts of failure many times trump our desire to try. Because of this, we remain in our habitual and debilitating patterns of our snug little comfort zone.

Contrary to what we are initially taught, failure is not the opposite of success but rather a crucial stepping stone toward it. Numerous inspiring stories of highly successful individuals highlight how failure is an integral part of their journey to success. Those who have achieved extraordinary feats in the world emphasize the significance of both learning from failures and using them as a springboard for growth.

We all love to talk about our success stories, but we're less likely to discuss our failures and roadblocks that were present and essential in reaching those success stories. Let's face it, as human beings; we don't like to be wrong, make mistakes, or look stupid. Those devious thought processes were planted into our brains when we were children. We were taught to be hyper-aware of the *perceptions of what others will think of us.* We have all subconsciously locked into those experiences of being laughed at when we floundered with an assignment in front of our grade school classmates.

In improv training, we develop a welcoming feeling towards our errors! Improv forces everyone to work as a team, and I don't know of any magical process that can accomplish that without making a few mistakes. Mistakes allow us to reconnect to our playful nature and embrace it as a welcome relief in our not having to "get it right" all the time.

Improv pushes us gently past our comfort zone and into the magnificent world of co-creation. By embracing and learning from our mistakes, we learn how to better connect, communicate, and collaborate under pressure.

When I conduct corporate training or lead an improv team retreat, I use exercises that force our critical thinking minds to step aside and, instead, trust our instincts – all without the fear of the need to "get it right." When we cheerfully experience the feeling of failing in an energetic, fun and supportive way, we discover how to abandon critical thinking and enjoy more stuff in life! We reorganize our relationship with mistakes by embracing them as essential learning opportunities, all in a climate of openness and kindness.

Celebrate yourself for the failures you have made (and will continue to make) because they validate the fact that you're a powerful risk-taking machine! Revelations!

Logic makes us think.
Emotion makes us act,
Emotion will always
trump logic!

— Joe Hammer

Chapter 3

Improv In Business Communications

Now that we have your brain tuned-up to the reality of how our thoughts can affect our behaviors, let's plug in some improv principles and techniques that can be applied to the world of business communications!

Active Listening

As I've previously mentioned, active listening is a communication skill that involves fully engaging with a speaker, understanding their message, and demonstrating attentiveness and empathy. This means being fully present in the moment, truly hearing and understanding what others are saying, seeking to understand their perspective. Active listening goes beyond simply hearing the words being spoken and encompasses a deeper level of understanding and connection. This is as critical in business communication as it is in an improv scene.

Improv performers must actively listen to their scene partners to understand the context of the scene and build on each other's ideas. They must be present and engaged in the moment, listening to what is being said and responding authentically. This allows them to create a cohesive and engaging scene.

Active listening is an essential component of effective business communication. By focusing on what the other person is saying, asking questions to clarify their meaning, and providing feedback, active listening can help build trust, understanding, and positive working relationships. Sadly, active listening is becoming a relic in today's world.

One of the popular improv games I use in my training is *String of Diamonds*, whereby a group of participants are lined up. The first person in the line starts a story with a simple opening sentence, such as, *"Once upon a time in a small village..."* while the last person in the line suggests a completely unrelated ending sentence, such as, *"... and that's when I realized I was aboard an alien aircraft."*

Now the story begins, with each participant adding a bit more information as it goes down the line. The aim of the game is to build a comprehensive story as it proceeds through the line of participants. Each must actively listen to the person before them, while "setting up" their next fellow participant, gently leading into a logical conclusion... in this example, as it relates to the alien aircraft.

Active listening is one of improv's foundational skills. Unlike *passive* listening, which is the act of hearing a speaker without retaining the full message, active listening permits engagement and recalling specific details without needing the information repeated.

Active listening involves *listening with all senses*. It is not on-ly essential in the world of improv, but it's also an influential tool for strong teammates, effective leaders and successful presenters. Developing this skill will help build and maintain relationships, solve problems, improve processes and retain information.

Sadly, however, most people aren't very good at active listen-ing. Most are listening to reply instead of listening to under-stand.

Let me say it again...

> *Most people are listening to reply instead of listening to understand.*

Attentive, active listening is a valuable skill in business, just as it is in a scene on the improv stage. Unfortunately, our clut-tered minds have reduced listening to simply *waiting for our turn to speak again*.

To successfully build a scene or conversation with a fellow player, we must actively listen to the offer they are giving us while integrating bits of it into our response. Many times, in an improv scene, a player will miss critical information that could have taken it to a more creative place. As a result of their oversight, the scene becomes boring, often frustrating to watch and many times annoying to fellow performers. If you are planning on what you "want to say" or "what you desire to happen," you will almost always miss out on important information. *You must attentively listen to what others are saying.*

When your team member, colleague, prospect or client recognizes that you're an active listener, they will feel more confident in taking their time when providing their information. This is because they know you aren't going to step on their words with unwelcomed interruptions. When you interrupt others, you are telling them you are either not listening, what they are saying is irrelevant to you, or you think your idea is better than theirs.

Collaborative relationships cannot be built on interruptions.

Active listening benefits us in our persuasion, influence, and rapport building skills. These skills are vital soft skills in today's business environment. As demonstrated in most every improv scene, the more we can link what we say in response to what another says, the more focused and directed the conversation will emerge.

Stay present in conversations. Make a conscious effort to commit to hearing and being respectful to your conversation partner. Be in the moment. Reflect on what was said *and reserve the urge to jump in too soon.* Pay attention to both verbal and non-verbal cues.

In my improv training, I developed an exercise called, *I heard You Say...* Two players engage in conversation, starting each of their sentences with "I heard you say," then repeats the information their fellow player just cited while adding additional supportive dialog to it...

Player #1: *"My dog has been itching a lot lately..."*

Player #2: *"I heard you say your dog has been itching a lot lately. You may consider bathing him in 'No More Itches' shampoo..."*

Player #1: *"I heard you say I should try 'No More Itches' shampoo..." that's a great idea. Maybe it'll work for me too, as I've been itching a lot..."*

Player #2: *"I heard you say you've been itching a lot ... perhaps YOU may have fleas..."*

Although this is obviously a humorous example of the exercise, it forces participants to actively listen, while still formulating short verbal responses.

In performances, I recommend players utilize this practice by connecting their partner's statements to their responses by using simple word connectors...

> *"I understand..."*
> *"I see..."*
> *"Yes, that makes sense..."*
> *"I agree..."*

These are all forms of positive responses, demonstrating you are listening.

Active Listening skills are advantageous, not only on the improv stage but in the corporate world as well. Because active listeners are highly engaged, they're better able to recall specific details in the communication process. The ability to clearly communicate instructions, ideas and concepts is truly a rare asset!

You will discover that the practice of improv principles also assists you in those often-uncomfortable, unarranged conversations that show up. From an unexpected question during a presentation to uninvited criticism, your knowledge of improv will position you to be in the right state of mind to handle the unexpected. You'll be grounded and credible instead of panic-stricken!

By listening actively to our colleagues, we can gain insight into their perspectives, priorities, and challenges, and use this information to work together more effectively towards shared goals. Active listening allows you to acknowledges and validates other's feelings, *"I can understand why you would feel frustrated by that."*

Whether you're on stage, interviewing for a new job, discussing a promotion, working with fellow team members, presenting information to an audience, or in a management role, improving active listening skills will assist you in more critical thinking and conflict resolution.

Let's look at some ways to be more present in the listening department...

Eliminating Distractions

When listening, eliminate as many distractions as possible. *Oh, and put away that damn phone.* Eliminating distractions can assist us in active listening by allowing us to focus our full attention on the person speaking, without any external factors interfering with our ability to process the message. By removing distractions and creating a quiet and focused environment, we can better concentrate on what our fellow communicator is saying, interpret their tone and body language, and respond in a more thoughtful and effective way. This can ultimately lead to better understanding, stronger relationships, and more productive outcomes in business communication.

Nonverbal Communication

Nonverbal cues in communication encompass the subtle signals and expressions we use to convey meaning without relying on words. These include facial expressions, body language, gestures, eye contact, tone of voice, and even personal space. They serve as powerful communicative tools, often complementing (but sometimes contradicting) the words we speak. Nonverbal cues can provide insights into emotions, intentions, attitudes, and relationships, adding depth to our interactions. By paying attention to these cues, we can better understand others and convey our own messages effectively, creating a richer and more nuanced form of communication.

Nodding your head, smiling, and using other nonverbal cues can help signal that you're actively listening and engaged with what others are saying. We'll go into great detail on Nonverbal Communication Techniques in Chapter 6, however I just want to touch base on this important communication aspect as it relates to active listening.

Make an effort to maintain eye contact throughout the conversation. It's powerful way to signal that you're fully engaged. When we make eye contact, we signal that we are fully present what others are saying. This encourages them to continue sharing their thoughts and ideas with us, leading to a more productive and meaningful conversation.

Failing to effectively use non-verbal cues can have the opposite effect, sometimes making others feel disrespected or unimportant. Two classic examples are looking away or checking your phone while someone is speaking. This sends a message that one is not interested in what another has to say.

Using non-verbal cues effectively can improve your active listening skills, enhance your communication with others, all while building stronger relationships. Again, more details on this masterful communication tool will be forthcoming!

Asking Questions

In most improv scenes, we try to steer clear of asking questions. The reason for this is that questions place the responsibility on our scene partner to come up with the information, which is really our job as a fellow scene performer. Rather than relying on them to provide the details, we need to contribute to the scene by building on the information they've already provided.

When it comes to business communications however, questions are an important element in the communication process. They serve as a powerful tool for demonstrating your interest in what others are saying, and for clarifying any points that may be unclear.

Asking questions demonstrates you are engaged and interested in the conversation. By asking open-ended questions, you encourage others to elaborate on their thoughts and feelings, giving you a better understanding of their perspective. This can help to build rapport and trust, as they feel their input is valued and respected. Some examples of open-ended questions:

> *"Can you give me a little more detail on that point you just made?"*
>
> *"Could you please clarify the timeline for this project?"*
>
> *"How do you handle conflict in the workplace?"*
>
> *"What are the biggest challenges you're facing right now that our product/service could help you solve?"*

It's common to make assumptions or jump to conclusions

during a conversation, however by asking questions, you can get a clearer picture of what others are attempting to convey. This can prevent misunderstandings and assist in ensuring that everyone is on the same page.

Questions can help to keep the conversation flowing and demonstrating that you are truly interested in hearing more. This encourages others to share additional information or insights, leading to a more productive and meaningful conversation.

Asking questions is an essential part of active listening and can significantly enhance the effectiveness of business communication.

Summarizing

After your conversation partner has finished making their point, summarize what they've said and paraphrase it back to them in your own words. This demonstrates that you've been actively listening and helps ensure that you've understood their perspective correctly. For example, you might say, *"So, what I'm hearing is that you need the report by Friday at noon and it should include projected revenue for the next quarter?"*

Summarizing is also an important skill in active listening because they demonstrate to others that you are engaged and have understood their message. When you restate their message in your own words, you clarify your understanding of the message, allowing them the opportunity to either confirm or correct your interpretation. I'll have more details about summarizing in the upcoming pages, along with several examples.

Being Prepared

Being prepared is essential in effective business communication. Know your subject matter well and have a detailed understanding of your team, prospects, clients or audiences as well as their needs. This will allow you to respond confidently and effectively to any unexpected questions or situations that may arise.

Diligent preparation also assists you in anticipating questions, reactions, and objections. By being prepared, you will project confidence, credibility, and competence, which can help to build trust and respect.

In improv, we use detailed initiating dialog to launch scenes. The better quality of the words and phrases we select will indeed reflect upon the quality of the scene that will emerge. Similarly, preparation is equally important when delivering presentations. A well-prepared presentation can capture and maintain attention, clarify complex information, and persuade taking action.

Being Flexible and Adaptable

This is the core benefit of using the principles of improv in business communication. Spontaneity involves being flexible and adaptable in response to unexpected situations. It will build trust, creativity, and innovation in the workplace. By being open to new ideas, taking calculated risks, and being open to stepping outside of your comfort zone, you will foster a culture of innovation and creativity. This will lead to more effective problem-solving, improved decision-making, and greater success in achieving goals and objectives.

Acceptance

Improv performers must accept whatever their scene partners offer, *even if it's not what they were expecting or hoping for*. This principle of acceptance is also relevant to business communication, as it means being open to different perspectives, ideas, and feedback. The direction of a sales presentation or team meeting very seldom goes as planned. By accepting input and ideas from others, you will build stronger relationships and foster a more collaborative work environment.

As improvisers, we do not judge ourselves or our scene partner's ideas. Instead, we focus on finding the truth "in the moment" while building a scene together. We embrace mistakes as opportunities to learn and grow. Mistakes very often lead to unexpected and interesting developments in the scene, creating a more authentic and engaging performance. These same elements of embracing acceptance relate to business communication, as they cultivate an open, non-judgmental mindset that values diverse perspectives and opinions.

Acceptance in business communication simply refers to the willingness to acknowledge and respect differing perspectives, opinions, and backgrounds. By accepting others' viewpoints, you will build trust, understanding, and positive relationships. You will foster a culture of inclusivity and diversity, leading to increased innovation, creativity, and problem-solving.

Approach every interaction with an open mind, and be willing to accept new ideas and perspectives!

Trust and Collaboration

Improv performers must trust their scene partners to support them and work together towards a common goal, that is, a successful and humorous scene. Collaboration ensures that scenes keep moving forward. Improvisers trust their instincts and take risks. If they have an idea that they believe could be funny or interesting, they go for it. In doing so they create a more engaging and dynamic scene.

In business communications, trust and collaboration are essential for achieving common goals, developing innovative solutions, and fostering a positive and productive work environment. By collaborating effectively, you will draw on each other's strengths, share resources, and achieve more than you could on your own.

So, you may be thinking... "Okay Joe, this all sounds good, but how does this active listening thing assist me in working with my clients, team members or prospects." Glad you asked my friend! Let's take a look at three areas where active listening will benefit your business communication efforts...

Building Relationships

Active listening is essential for building strong relationships with colleagues, clients, and prospective clients. It does so by fostering understanding, trust, and connection. It conveys that their opinions matter to you, which helps create a sense of value and importance in the relationship. This can help you tailor your communication to better meet their needs, whether it's in a sales presentation, negotiation, or a project management team meeting.

Active listening encourages empathy by allowing you to see the world from the other person's point of view. It helps you relate to their emotions, challenges, and joys. This empathy fosters compassion and a genuine care for other's well-being.

Resolving Conflicts

Active listening is essential for resolving conflicts in the workplace by providing an opportunity for all parties to express their concerns and perspectives. It allows for a deeper understanding of each other's needs and motivations, facilitating a collaborative approach to finding solutions. Additionally, active listening helps prevent misunderstandings by giving space to clarify and seek clarification before assumptions escalate.

By fully understanding each of our colleagues' perspective and concerns, everyone will find common ground and work together to find a solution that meets all's needs. Misunderstandings can lead to costly mistakes and damaged relationships. Active listening can help to avoid misunderstandings by ensuring that you fully understand the other person's message and can clarify any points of confusion.

Improving Productivity

When you actively listen , you can better understand the task at hand and any challenges or obstacles that may arise. This can help you to work more efficiently and effectively, leading to increased productivity and better outcomes.

Pay attention to the person speaking and focus on their words, tone, and body language. Physically be present in the meeting. Engage with your team members by making eye contact, nodding, or giving nonverbal cues to show that you are paying attention. Focusing on your team members during meetings is essential for effective communication. Again, I'll have more on these effective communication tools in Chapter 6.

The Tools of Active Listening

Now that you have been made aware of the importance of active listening. Let's take a look at a few techniques to help you become a proficient active listener in the realm of business communications:

Be Present

Avoid multitasking during the meeting. Instead, focus solely on the meeting and what is being discussed. Encourage participation from all team members by giving everyone a chance to speak and share their ideas. Make eye contact and avoid distractions. This creates a more collaborative environment where everyone feels heard and valued.

Avoid Interrupting

Reflect on your communication habits and identify if inter-rupting is a common behavior for you. Recognizing this tendency is the first step towards making positive changes. Work on your patience and remind yourself to listen fully before responding. Avoid interrupting your team member when they are talking, *even if you have a pressing idea or comment to add.* Instead, wait for them to finish speaking before sharing your thoughts. Allow others to finish express-ing their thoughts and ideas. Give them the time and space they need to communicate their message.

It is natural for us to instinctively pause to gather our thoughts or take a breath. Use these moments to respond or ask questions. Waiting for appropriate breaks in the conversa-tion ensures that you are not cutting off others.

Exercise self-control and refrain from interjecting or speaking over others. Remind yourself of the importance of giving each person an opportunity to express themselves fully. Remem-ber, effective communication involves both listening and speaking. By practicing active listening by consciously avoid-ing interruptions, you create an environment that promotes understanding, respect, and collaborative communication.

Repeat What You Heard

As previously mentioned, summarize what others have said to ensure you understood their message correctly. This demonstrates that you are actively listening, engaged and interested in understanding their perspective. Ask questions to clarify any points that are unclear or to gain more information. Further, asking questions to clarify points made by your team members can help ensure everyone is on the same page and avoid misunderstandings. Some examples:

"Can you explain that further?" This question allows the speaker to expand on their point and provide more details.

"What do you mean by...?" This question helps to clarify any specific terminology or jargon that may be unclear.

"How do you find that relates to...?" This question helps to connect the speaker's point to a larger context or goal.

"Can you provide an example?" This question allows the speaker to provide a concrete example to illustrate their point.

"What do you believe to be the main takeaways?" This question helps to summarize the key points made by the speaker and ensure everyone understands the main message.

Provide Feedback

Providing feedback to your team members demonstrates that you were actively listening and acknowledging their contribution. Providing responses to comments or suggestions made by others is vital for collaboration.

Always start with *positive* feedback. Begin by acknowledging what you liked or appreciated about the comment or suggestion made by your team member. This helps to create a positive and supportive environment for discussion. Express what you found helpful or valuable about the comment or suggestion. This allows your team member to understand what they did well and encourages them to continue contributing.

If there are areas where you think the comment or suggestion could be improved, gently offer specific suggestions for how to do so. Be sure to provide constructive comments rather than simply criticizing or dismissing the idea.

Any time you are unsure about a comment or suggestion, *ask for clarification.* This shows that you are interested in understanding the idea and encourages open and honest communication. End your feedback by reiterating the positive aspects of the comment or suggestion and expressing your appreciation for your team member's contribution.

By following these tips, you can provide feedback to your team members in a way that promotes open communication and collaboration, while also encouraging constructive feedback and improvement.

Now that you've hyper-groomed your active listening skills, let's move on to the next core concept of effective improv, the *"Yes, and..."*principle...

Yes, and...

Comedic improv has a few simple rules that must be followed to allow scenes to unfold into improvised masterpieces. The most famous is the *"Yes, and....."* rule, or the *Rule of Agreement*.

This rule suggests that players must:

1. *Agree with the reality their scene partner is creating,* and

2. *Add additional detailed information to that reality.*

An example of "Yes, and..."agreement dialog between players:

Player #1: *"I can't believe we got stranded on this deserted island."*

Player #2: *"Yes, and... it looks like we're the only ones here."*

Player #1: *"Yes, and... if we're going to survive, we'll need to find food and shelter."*

Player #2: *"Yes, and... let's start by building a shelter out of these palm fronds."*

Player #1: *"Yes, and... maybe we could open those coconuts for water."*

Player #2: *"Yes, and... I think we can catch some fish for dinner."*

In this example, each player is saying "yes" to their partner's ideas and building upon them to create a collaborative scene. They accept the reality of the situation presented by their partner and add to it in a way that moves the scene forward.

If a fellow player rejects the other player's reality, the scene will stagnate and becomes stymied by conflict. For example,

>**Player #1:** *"I can't believe we got stranded on this deserted island."*
>
>**Player #2:** *"We're not on a deserted island, we're at the beach."*

This is referenced as *denying* or *blocking* in the improv world (I'll have more on this later).

It does nothing to move the scene forward, creates friction between players and has no place to go.

No matter how bizarre or outlandish it may be, improv players are obligated and honored to accept their fellow player's dialog and boldly move the scene forward.

For example, if one player says, *"I think we should climb that mountain,"* the other player might respond with *"Yes, and... we should bring some energy bars to eat along the way."*

A response to, *"Wow, this is a beautiful beach,"* could be, *"Yes, and... I can't believe how soft the white sand is."*

In improv, the "Yes, and..." rule helps to establish a positive and supportive environment where every idea is valued, and the improvisers are encouraged to take risks and contribute to the scene.

We must use this same "Yes, and..."principle in our business communication. We must agree with our colleague, team member, prospect or client during our communication process. By doing so, this positive response acknowledges and builds upon the original idea, keeping the conversation moving forward and allowing for more creativity and collaboration.

The "Yes, and..."principle is applicable in business communications for a number of reasons. Firstly, it encourages active listening and engagement with others. Instead of focusing on your own ideas or agenda, you are fully present in the moment and focused on building something together with your prospect, client or team member.

Secondly, "Yes, and..."creates a sense of trust and safety. When you know that your ideas will be accepted and built upon, you are more likely to take risks and share your own ideas. This can lead to more creative and innovative solutions, as well as stronger team dynamics.

By accepting and building on each other's contributions, you are demonstrating a willingness to learn and grow together. In a business setting, innovation and adaptability are keys to success.

Using the "Yes, and..."principle encourages team members to listen to each other's ideas, and build on them to create innovative solutions to complex problems. It creates a collaborative environment where everyone's ideas are valued. And, by adding new information, keeps the communication process moving forward in a positive way.

Acknowledge the strength of ideas brought forward, as well as the value it could bring to the project or initiative. That's the *"Yes"* part.

Now build on the idea by suggesting additional ways to improve it or take it to the next level. That's the *"and..."* Be specific and provide concrete examples of how other's suggestions could enhance the original idea.

I know what you're thinking, saying "yes" to a statement may thrust you into a quick, unknown future, a leap of faith into the abyss of uncertainty, right? No, it actually doesn't. I'll have a few examples in a moment.

If you really think about it, exercising the "yes muscle" is an act of bravery and optimism. In uttering an affirming "yes" statement, you share control of the conversation with your partner, while making them happy in return! *Our brains actually enjoy saying "yes" to new discoveries!*

Beyond the standard "Yes and," response, there are other offers of agreement that are just as effective...

"You bet..."

"You're right..."

"Sure..."

"Okay..."

"Of course..."

"I'm with you..."

"Good idea..."

We'll delve into examples of this in business communications in just a moment, but for now, just understand that *it's not cool to negate.* We've been denied enough in life, so there really isn't a need to bring "no" into our communications. Instead, discover and exercise the power of "Yes!"

Once embracing the "Yes, and..."Rule of Agreement with like-minded colleagues, you'll discover how the power of affirmatively working together spills over into your everyday life. Whether in a staff meeting or on stage, agreeing with your partner, team member or colleague begins a *building* process.

Great improvisers joyfully let go of the future and focus on being present in the moment. By doing so, they learn to disregard one of our most fundamental human instincts, *they avoid thinking ahead.* Due to the ever-changing scene environment in improv, *there is no future.* Well, there is, but we just don't know what it entails! A good improv scene is like a game of ping pong... without the points. You serve, they return. They serve, you return.

It's about confidence. Confidence in team efforts. Think about it... people who aren't confident seldom contribute, so everyone loses. When you habitually meet situations with an energetic "yes," the mysterious energy of agreement transforms the way people perceive you. Confidence is quickly amplified. It's about a new *infrastructure* of communicating and connecting.

To experience the power of "Yes, and..." in your life, select a person you know and care for to experiment with. Choose to say YES and agree to everything for a full week. Agree with all of their statements, ideas or recommendations. Consider their thoughts and opinions ahead of your own. This will assist you in becoming more creative with your answers. If you truly disagree with a statement made by another, by first agreeing you'll find your disagreement being eventually addressed but in a more pleasant, non-adversarial and distinctive way!

For example, if a friend offers you a huge piece of chocolate cake on the first day of your diet, your response could be, *"Thank you! I've just started my new diet, however I'll put this in the fridge for my very first cheat day... I'm looking forward to it!"*

This is an affirmative approach. No denying. No refusal. Don't you agree that it's a better response than, *"No thanks, I'm on a diet."*

Powerful life lessons are built into the "Yes, and..."rule. The next time someone shares their idea with you, remain open-minded and accept it. Even if you find fault with it, begin by accepting it as viable, and *then add to it.* Saying "yes" keeps us open to possibilities and with more possibilities, we discover limitations are removed!

So, now you know… the number one rule in improv is the "Yes, and…"rule. Through the pillar of acceptance, you establish trust and mutual respect. Just as in life and business, quick adaptation to ever-changing criteria, finicky clients and a demanding boss are all commonplace. Always strive to build on another's ideas and offer suggestions!

Here are some examples of the "Yes and…" improv principle and how it applies to not necessarily "accepting" everything another may be expressing, but instead *accepting their input in a way that can lead to agreement.…*

> *"Yes, and… I think your proposal could help us streamline our workflow. Let's look at how we can integrate it into our existing processes."*

In this example, one is not agreeing with the proposal, but instead looking at possibilities of further reviewing and possibly integrating it.

> *"Yes, and… I appreciate your insights on market trends. Let's brainstorm some strategies to capitalize on those trends and improve our sales numbers."*

In this example, one is not agreeing with the insights, but instead looking at possibilities of further brainstorming their ideas.

"Yes, and... I think your feedback on the design is valuable. Let's see how we can incorporate those suggestions and make the product more user-friendly."

In this example, one is not agreeing with their design recommendations, but instead looking at further exploring their feedback as it relates to the design.

"Yes, and... I agree that we need to address customer complaints. Let's work together to come up with a solution that satisfies their needs and improves our reputation."

In this example, one is not dismissing their recommendations, but instead looking at further exploring solutions to customer complaints.

In all of these examples, the listener is simply acknowledging another's contribution and demonstrating *a willingness to work together to achieve a common goal.* This creates a positive and collaborative work environment that leads to better outcomes and stronger team relationships.

Here are some examples of how to use the "Yes, and..." principle of improv in common, yet sometimes challenging business communication scenarios:

Brainstorming

When brainstorming with your team, use the "Yes, and..." principle to build on each other's ideas. When someone presents an idea, accept it with a "yes" and then add your own contribution with an "and." The goal is to create an environment where everyone feels comfortable sharing their ideas, and where each idea is built upon to generate even more innovative solutions.

At the beginning of the brainstorming session, be sure to establish ground rules that encourages everyone to participate and build on each other's ideas. For example, you might set a rule that no idea is too small or too crazy, or that everyone should try to contribute at least one idea.

When someone presents an idea, start by saying "yes" to show that you are open to their idea. Even if you don't fully agree with the idea or think it's the best solution, it's important to acknowledge and accept it before moving on.

After saying "yes," add the "and" to build upon the idea. For example, if someone suggests a new marketing campaign, you might say, *"Yes, and... we could leverage social media influencers to help promote it."*

After you have added your own "and," encourage others to do the same. This helps to build momentum and generate even more ideas. As you move through the brainstorming session, continue to build on the previous ideas with the "Yes, and..." approach. This helps to create continuity and progress in the brainstorming process.

Problem Solving

Use the "Yes, and..."principle to approach problems with a

collaborative mindset. Instead of shooting down ideas, accept them with a "yes" and then build on them with an "and" to find a solution that works for everyone.

When using this principle in problem-solving with your team members, the goal is to create an environment where everyone feels comfortable sharing their ideas and building upon each other's solutions.

Start by defining the problem you want to solve. Make sure everyone is clear on what the problem is and what the desired outcome is. Encourage your team members to come up with solutions to the problem. Use the "Yes, and..." principle to build on each other's ideas and create a collaborative environment.

Remember to accept and build on each other's ideas *without judgment.*

Once you have a list of potential solutions, evaluate each one based on its feasibility and effectiveness. Again, use the "Yes, and..." principle to build on each other's evaluations and opinions. After evaluating the potential solutions, choose the best one. Again use the "Yes, and..."principle to continue to build on the chosen solution and refine it as necessary.

Once a solution is reached, assign tasks and responsibilities to team members to ensure that the solution is implemented effectively.

Supportive Teamwork

Use the "Yes, and..."principle to create a supportive and collaborative team environment. Encourage team members to accept each other's ideas and build on them to achieve common goals. By actively listening to your team members and accepting their ideas with a "yes," you create an atmosphere of respect and trust. This can lead to better communication and a more productive team. Using the "Yes, and..."Rule of Agreement approach encourages team members to take risks and try new things. Everyone's ideas are valued and team members are more likely to take risks and explore new ideas.

Difficult Conversations and Conflict Resolutions

The "Yes, and..."principle can be applied in difficult conversations to create a more constructive and collaborative environment. It involves acknowledging and validating the other person's perspective, finding common ground, building on each other's ideas, being open to feedback, and focusing on solutions. These techniques can help to shift the conversation from blame or criticism to finding a solution, which can ultimately lead to better results for everyone.

By acknowledging and validating the other person's perspective, you demonstrate that you understand and respect their point of view. Finding common ground helps identify shared goals and creates a sense of collaboration.

Being open to feedback can help to create a more constructive and supportive environment that fosters growth and development. And focusing on solutions can help to shift the conversation from a negative to a positive tone, which can ultimately lead to better outcomes for everyone.

Team Building Activities

The "Yes, and..."Rule of Agreement is a dynamic tool for team building. Incorporating improv exercises into team building activities can promote collaboration, creativity, and active listening.

Building trust within the team is another area where "Yes, and..."can be useful. Encouraging team members to take risks and try new things knowing their ideas will be acknowledged and built upon can create a positive and supportive team environment. By using the "Yes, and..."improv technique, you will discover it to be a powerful tool for improving team efforts in business communications.

Introduce the rule to your team. Explain to everyone that the goal is to build upon each other's ideas and create a positive and supportive environment. Encourage active listening. Emphasize its importance and advise team members to fully listen to each other's contributions without judgment or interruption. Encourage them to accept and acknowledge each other's ideas and contributions. Instead of dismissing or criticizing ideas, they should focus on finding value in them.

After acknowledging an idea, advise team members to build upon it by adding their own contributions. This can be done by expanding on the initial idea, offering alternative perspectives, or suggesting complementary concepts.

After engaging in team-building activities using the "Yes, and..."principle, reflect on the experience. Discuss the impact it had on the team's collaboration, creativity, and problem-solving abilities. Identify any challenges faced and brainstorm ways to overcome them.

The "Yes, and..."rule centers on a mindset of acceptance, openness, and collaboration. By integrating this approach into your team-building efforts, you can cultivate a positive team culture that nurtures creativity, enhances communication, and fosters stronger relationships among team members!

Dreaded Denials

The opposite of the "Yes, and..."rule is that of a *denial*. Improv scenes avoid denials. Denials (sometimes called "blocking") refers to the act of rejecting or dismissing a fellow player's offers or ideas during a scene.

Player #1: *"I can't believe we got stranded on this deserted island."*

Player #2: *"It's not a deserted island. It's a mirage."*

Player #1: *"It's definitely an island; see the water, sand and trees?"*

Player #2: *"No, it looks more like a desert and that water is fake."*

In this example, improviser #2 denies the reality of the situation presented by their partner. This leads to conflict, slowing or halting of the scene. By denying their partner's ideas, denials create a negative and unproductive environment that discourages creativity and innovation.

In business communications, denials can terminate a conversation. They can also create tension and conflict among those participating in the conversation, which can make it difficult to establish a collaborative and supportive environment.

In business communication, I reference denials as *non-supportive language.*

Saying "no" is the ego's way of attempting to manage the future. It's our brain's historic way of trying to *control* the situation instead of *accepting* it. Many people are so used to saying "no" that it has developed into a standard reaction!

The moment you break the "Yes, and..." Rule of Acceptance, the action ends. For example:

> **Player #1:** *"Hey Mike, let's go to the water park today; it's half price Monday!"*

> **Player #2:** *"No, I don't like water parks."*

Player #2 just killed the scene; there's no place to go. It's their inner critic offensively desiring to have it "their" way.

We block when:

- we say no

- we think we have a better idea

- we fail to actively listen

- we simply ignore a given element in a conversation

Blocking surfaces when the detractor in us attempts to take over the conversation. In many cases, it's an ego-centered response.

The "Yes, and..." Rule of Acceptance declares that no matter what happens on stage during an improv scene, each player must accept it as real. We don't have to like it or believe it, but it's our obligation to *accept* it. It's not where we think a scene *should* go, but the acceptance that's required to allow it to go *where it is going.* Saying "yes" and following through with added information to move the scene forward prevents us from blocking.

The same thing rings true in business communications. For example, when a team member suggests an idea during a brainstorming session, it is often denied without considering its merits or offering an explanation... *"That won't work. We've tried it before, and it didn't succeed."*

Another form of denial is failing to acknowledge or address another's input or suggestion, *"We'll take that into consideration later. Let's move on..."*

Other times when denials are present:

Shutting down or refusing to collaborate or engage in joint problem-solving efforts, *"Thanks, but I prefer working on this project alone."*

Reacting defensively or dismissively to feedback or constructive criticism, *"I don't agree with your position on the matter. I think my approach is better."*

Blocking new perspectives by disregarding ideas or opinions that challenge the status quo, *"We've always done it this way, and I don't see a reason to change now."*

Undermining suggestions by pointing out potential obstacles or problems without offering any alternative solutions *"That idea won't work because we don't have the budget or the resources."*

These examples highlight instances where the "Yes, and…"rule is violated in business communications, hindering collaboration, creativity, and open dialogue. By recognizing and addressing these denials, teams can foster a more inclusive, supportive, and innovative work environment.

Denials in Life

Denial is many times the result of a bad decision. Don't be stuck living in denial. You can always make more affirmative decisions. Just as we do in an improv scene, be willing to accept what is put before you, and build upon it.

Denials have become easy to dole out as we have experienced a lot of negativities in our lives. A UCLA survey found that the average one-year-old child hears the word 'No' more than 400 times a day! This may sound like an exaggeration, but it's not. Actually, when we tell a toddler "No," we often say, "No, no, no!" which is accentuating the negative message three times in seconds! If you were an active, curious, inquisitive and daring child like I was, you likely heard it even more! Misdirected childhood experiences have resulted in many undesired consequences in our adult lives.

Don't be the person who finds "no" a viable or conditioned response. Just as we do in improv, observe how you not only speak to your children, your partner, or your fellow workers but also how you speak to yourself - inside your own head. Be positive and inspiring. Those who find "Yes" to be a more suitable response are rewarded by adventures. Those who say "No" merely remain with the safety they were already experiencing. There's no fun in that.

As improvisers, we avoid denials at all costs. You should too.

> DON'T BE THE PERSON WHO FINDS "NO" A VIABLE OR CONDITIONED RESPONSE.

Seedy Shut Downs

Now, let's look at how we may respond by using denials as a "but" in business communication.

> *Ya gotta keep your "but" outta the conversation.*
> - Joe Hammer

There is a communication element in business communications that negates a positive result. I refer to it as a "shutdown" because it truly does shut down the communication process.

Think about the last time you offered your input, opinion or thoughts in a conversation only to find it dismissed, ignored, refused or simply unacknowledged. Did you feel the desire to offer more feedback? Heck no! Our brain naturally says, *"Well, they don't want to hear what I have to say, so I'll shut up and stay out of the conversation."*

Some examples of shut downs...

"No, I don't think that's a good idea. We should stick to our existing processes."

"I disagree. I don't think that strategy is viable given our current resources."

"Thanks, but I think the design is fine as it is."

"I don't think the complaints are that significant. We should focus on other priorities."

In these examples, one shuts down their colleague's ideas without showing a willingness to work collaboratively towards a shared goal. This can create a negative and unproductive work environment that most always leads to poor outcomes and weaker team relationships.

We tend to nurture the default response of "yes, but..." instead of "Yes, and..."In doing so, we reject, contradict, or, in the worst case, ignore our partner's offer.

In improv training, I refer to the "yes, but" response as a "denial in a tuxedo" as it first appears to be supportive, but actually takes an undesirable shift when the recipient of the message quickly recognizes their input has been rejected.

To truly communicate, *connection* is required. We must let go of our initial opinion and really engage with what others are bringing to the table. There are four primary steps to shift off your but...

Magnify your awareness. Accept as many suggestions, offers and propositions as possible. Be in the presence of mind to actively listen. Peek beyond the words spoken and identify the emotions, values, and deeper interests that exist. *Effective leadership requires attentiveness.*

Say "yes" to what's offered. Use the "Yes, and..."principle, accepting what others are contributing. Remember that doing so doesn't mean you fully agree with what they have provided; it simply means accepting their *input* - without avoiding, ignoring, dismissing or invalidating it. Yes Grasshopper, this requires setting your ego and agenda aside.

Paraphrase what you've heard. Before moving on, summarize what you've heard and be sure your team members are satisfied that you truly understood their contribution.

Add to what's emerging. Consider how you can build on the information offered. Perhaps ask a question to identify more details about their vision and add additional details to their offer.

Begin approaching every conversation and team meeting interaction as an opportunity to improvise. You and your team will cover more ground while experiencing a greater degree of cooperation and imagination. And don't deny.

Denials are often perceived as an attack on the other person, who feels their idea is being dismissed or of no value.

Chapter 4

Creating a Supportive Culture
The Desire to Feel Safe

In teaching improv, a safe and supportive environment is a prerequisite to learning. Because without a safe environment, class members can feel as nervous as a cat in a room full of rocking chairs!

Encourage your team members to share their thoughts and ideas openly, without fear of judgment or criticism. Model respectful communication and behavior, while making it clear that disrespectful behavior will not be tolerated. When providing feedback, focus on constructive suggestions, aimed at helping team members improve. Avoid personal attacks and "shooting down" ideas.

In effective business communication, the establishment of clear guidelines is the first step. These guidelines must outline what is expected of participants in terms of respect, support, and collaboration. Further, you must ensure that everyone understands and agrees to these guidelines to maintain a positive and inclusive culture where everyone is valued and respected, regardless of their backgrounds, experiences, or abilities.

Encouraging Openness

Encouraging open communication during meetings is essential to creating an environment that fosters collaboration and innovation. Advise team members to actively listen to each other and communicate clearly and effectively. This is as essential in creating a supportive business environment as it is for a sometimes-daunting first-time improv class. When participants are actively engaged in listening and communicating with one another, it creates an environment where everyone feels heard and valued.

Taking creative risks is an integral part of improv, so creating an environment that encourages participants to take those risks is crucial for personal and team growth. Celebrating mistakes and converting failures to opportunities for learning and growth will also help participants feel more comfortable taking risks and exploring their creativity.

Let your team members know that their opinions and ideas are valued and that they are free to express themselves without fear of judgment or ridicule. Make it a safe place!

Setting the Tone

If you are leading your group, it's important to set the tone for the meeting. Start by acknowledging everyone at the meeting and creating a welcoming atmosphere. Explain the purpose of the meeting and why it is important to have ground rules. Keep the ground rules simple and easy to understand. Some examples:

- Respect everyone's opinions and ideas
- Avoid interrupting others while they are speaking
- Stay focused on the topic at hand
- Be open-minded and willing to consider different perspectives
- Avoid using negative or confrontational language
- Listen actively and avoid side conversations
- Maintain confidentiality when discussing sensitive information

Remember, the goal of setting ground rules is to create a supportive and productive environment for the team to work together towards a common goal. Remind everyone that failure is an opportunity to learn and grow. They must recognize and understand that failure is a natural part of the learning process and that it's okay to make mistakes. This will help everyone understand the importance of the rules and why they are being set.

Sharing

Encourage everyone to share their thoughts and ideas. Advise them you (as well as other team members) will be attentive and will indeed value their contributions. This will encourage others to speak up as well. Make sure that everyone has an opportunity to contribute. Encourage those who may be more introverted or hesitant to share their thoughts by specifically asking for their input.

Always allow your team members to finish their thoughts before responding. Interrupting can make people feel dismissed or unimportant. Encourage them to share their unique perspectives

INTERRUPTING CAN MAKE PEOPLE FEEL DISMISSED OR UNIMPORTANT.

and opinions. Again, acknowledge and validate their contributions, *even if you don't agree with them.*

Utilize the power of Active Listening as discussed in the previous chapter. Pay attention to what your team members are saying and show that you are listening by nodding, maintaining eye contact, and asking questions to clarify points.

Solution Seeking

When discussing issues or problems, avoid blaming individuals or criticizing their ideas. Instead, focus on finding solutions together. Use language that's neutral and focuses on the issue rather than the person. Instead of saying, *"you didn't do this"* or *"you made a mistake"* you can say *"this didn't seem to go as planned"* or *"we encountered a challenge in this area."*

It's important to approach the conversation with a problem-solving mindset rather than a blaming mindset. Ask open-ended questions and actively listening to your team members' perspectives. Everyone must feel comfortable sharing their ideas and opinions without fear of judgment or reprisal.

Using Positive Language

Use positive language to encourage and motivate your team members. Instead of saying, *"That won't work,"* say, *"That's an interesting idea. Let's explore it further."* Some other examples of the use of positive language:

"That's a great point, and I think we could build on that idea to…"

"I appreciate your perspective, and I think it adds valuable insight to the discussion."

"I agree with your suggestion, and let's explore it further to see how we can implement it."

"I'm glad we have a team that can bring diverse ideas to the table, and I believe we can come up with a solution that benefits everyone."

"Thank you for sharing your thoughts. Let's brainstorm together to see how we can make this work."

"I think we're making great progress as a team, and I'm excited to see where this discussion leads us."

"It's great to see everyone working together and collaborating towards a common goal."

Using positive language compliments a safe and open environment for business communication that's crucial to ensuring that everyone feels comfortable to express themselves and contribute effectively. It fosters trust, respect, and collaboration among team members, leading to better communication, increased creativity, and improved problem-solving.

Open Communications

Open communication is essential for building trust and nurturing collaboration in the workplace. This includes regular meetings, progress updates, and feedback sessions between team members, departments, and management. When conflicts arise - and they will - it's important to address them in a collaborative and constructive way. By listening to all sides of the issue and working together to find a solution, team members can build trust and strengthen their working relationships.

By providing constructive feedback and actively listening to feedback from others, team members can build trust and improve their communication and collaboration skills. Open communications will enable your team to rely on one another and share ideas without fear of judgement or criticism.

The Practice of Empathy

Make an effort to understand others' perspectives, experiences, and emotions. Put yourself in their shoes and consider their unique circumstances, challenges, and motivations.

Imagine yourself in their position. Try to view situations from their viewpoint. This helps develop a deeper understanding of their needs, motivations, and reactions. This will assist you in connecting with them and responding in a more thoughtful and empathetic way.

Give colleagues your full attention. Maintain eye contact and show genuine interest in what they have to say. Avoid interrupting or formulating responses before they finish speaking. Respond with empathy and understanding. Validate their feelings and experiences, even if you don't agree with them. Use phrases like, *"I understand how you feel,"* or *"That sounds challenging."*

Acknowledge and appreciate the contributions and efforts of your colleagues. Recognize their achievements publicly as well as privately. Small gestures of gratitude can go a long way in building empathy and positive relationships. Be available to lend a helping hand or provide support when others are facing challenges or going through difficult times.

Practicing empathy allows you to better understand their perspective, and responding in a way that shows you care about their feelings and needs.

Using "I" Statements

When expressing your perspective, use "I" or "I feel" statements over often accusatory statements beginning with "you."

This demonstrates that you're taking ownership of your own feelings and not blaming others. *"I can understand why you might feel that way"* demonstrates that you are actively trying to understand another's viewpoint and can help to foster more effective communication. Here are some examples of challenging "you" centered statements compared to more effective "I" centered options:

Instead of, *"You always make mistakes in your work."*

Try, *"I believe we can enhance the quality of our work by focusing on identifying areas for improvement and implementing strategies for growth."*

Instead of, *"You need to fix this immediately."*

Try, *"I suggest we address this matter promptly to ensure a smooth workflow and meet our objectives effectively."*

Instead of, *"You don't understand what we're trying to achieve."*

Try, *"I would like to provide more clarity on our goals and objectives to ensure we are aligned and working together towards a common purpose."*

Instead of, *"You should have known better."*

Try, *"I believe we can learn from this situation and find opportunities for growth and improvement moving forward."*

Avoiding "you" centered statements by replacing them with "I" centered options will help convey empathy and understanding towards others' perspectives.

Practicing Active Kindness

Similar to active listening, *active kindness* is simply intentional acts of kindness and compassion towards others. It involves actively seeking opportunities to assist, support, or uplift others, rather than just reacting to situations when they arise.

In improv, we strive to have our fellow team players' backs. That is, we seek to make our troupe members look great. They, in turn, do the same for us. We practice kindness, even when our improv characters seek conflict with our fellow player's characters! It's never personal.

Active kindness involves us making a conscious effort to make the world a better place by helping those around us. Show kindness and respect to others in your communications, even during difficult situations.

Active kindness goes beyond simply being nice or polite in a passive or reactive manner. It involves consciously and purposefully taking actions to help, support, or uplift others without expecting anything in return.

Those irritating people around you are just teachers sent by the Universe to educate a stubborn student.

— Joe Hammer

Chapter 5

Building on Ideas and Contributions

The "Suggestion"

In the context of improv, "suggestions" refer to ideas offered by audience members to inspire our scenes. These suggestions serve as a starting point for improvisers to build upon and create spontaneous content. These can be as simple as a word or phrase, or as complex as a full scenario, such as *"The First Date from Hell"* whereby two people are on their first date, but things don't go as planned. Or perhaps, *"Time Travel Mix-Up,"* where players travel through time, but end up in a completely different location than they intended. By using audience suggestions, improvisers tap into the collective creativity of their fellow team members and create scenes that are unique, interesting, and unexpected.

This concept of building upon other people's ideas is just as important in business meetings as it is in improv. It's an essential skill leading to collaboration, innovation, and better outcomes. We must pay attention to what the person is saying, asking questions to clarify their perspective, and show a genuine interest in their idea.

In brainstorming sessions or problem-solving discussions, team members must offer suggestions to generate ideas and solutions. These suggestions act as starting points for exploration and creativity, opening up possibilities that may not have been considered otherwise.

Suggestions also foster collaboration and encourage diverse perspectives. By inviting input and ideas from team members, you create a space for innovative thinking and fresh insights. Each suggestion can be built upon or combined with others to develop stronger and more comprehensive approaches.

Encouraging suggestions during meetings empowers everyone to contribute and actively engage. It creates a sense of ownership and involvement, leading to a more inclusive and participatory work environment. When faced with challenges or obstacles, suggestions from team members will provide alternative viewpoints and potential solutions.

In performance evaluations or feedback sessions, suggestions can be offered constructively to help individuals improve their skills, processes, or outcomes. Offering actionable suggestions in a supportive manner helps foster growth and development within the team.

Suggestions also encourage open-minded approaches to new ideas, market trends, and client feedback. By considering and incorporating relevant suggestions, companies will stay agile and adapt to changing circumstances more effectively.

Finally, in client interactions, actively soliciting suggestions or feedback can demonstrate a commitment to listening and understanding their needs.

As you can see, suggestions have their place not only on the improv stage, but in business communications as well!

Use Supportive Language

Again, avoid denials and "buts." Denials create confusion and conflict in a conversation. They are detrimental to the flow and energy of effective communications. It can also create conflict or tension that can be challenging to resolve.

Using supportive language is crucial for building positive relationships and creating a productive work environment. It involves using language that's respectful, empathetic, and constructive.

Start by acknowledging the perspectives and ideas of your team members. Actively listen to what they have to say and responding in a way that demonstrates understanding and respect. For example, use phrases like, *"I see where you're coming from,"* or *"That's an interesting point."* Doing so shows that you value the opinions of others and are open to different perspectives!

Avoid negative or judgmental language by refraining from saying things that are critical, dismissive, or disrespectful. Instead, focus on language that's positive and constructive. For example, if someone suggests an idea, instead of saying, *"That won't work,"* say, *"That's an interesting idea. Let's explore it further and see how we can make it work."*

Much better, right?

Use "we" language when talking about team efforts. Doing so will create a sense of inclusivity and collaboration. For example, *"Yes, let's work together to brainstorm some solutions to this problem"* or *"Yes, I'm sure we can achieve this goal by collaborating."*

Supportive language offers solutions over criticism and creates a more positive and supportive work environment. Don't focus on the problems or shortcomings. Instead, offer solutions and suggestions for how to improve the situation or subject at hand.

Again, recognize and appreciate the efforts and accomplishments of others.

Provide Examples

Examples can help illustrate your point and make your ideas more tangible. This can also help your team members better understand how their ideas can be applied in real-world situations. They are an effective way to clarify and support your ideas. Make sure they are directly related to the point you are making. If possible, use "real-world" personal examples as they can help humanize the message and make it more relatable. Sharing personal experiences will assist in building trust and rapport with your team members.

Don't get bogged down in unnecessary details. In improv, we call needless babbling on stage as *monologuing*. We strive to keep our dialog simple, succinct and to the point so our fellow players can easily follow along. Keep your points short and sweet. Small chunks of information are better assimilated than endless bantering. Use descriptive language to paint a picture in your team members' minds. This can help them visualize the story and remember it more easily.

Improv players also practice *specificity*, which means that incorporating specific details into their dialogue can enhance the quality of their performance. For instance, consider a scene where I observe a giraffe in my neighbor's backyard. Simply saying, *"Look, there's a giraffe in your backyard,"* is intriguing, but adding descriptive elements like, *"Look! There's a giraffe eating all the apples off your apple tree!"* adds depth and richness to the scene.

However, it's important to strike a balance because providing excessive information can hinder my scene partner's ability to respond effectively. For example, saying, *"Look! There's a giraffe eating all the apples off your apple tree. I bet it got loose from the zoo. I sure hope we don't also have elephants and monkeys showing up in our yard!"* This overwhelms the scene with too much information, making it a challenge for my scene partner to determine the main focus of the statement. If referencing a story, make sure it is relevant to the topic and has a clear and simple beginning, middle and end. This will help your team members follow along and understand the message you are trying to convey.

Employ analogies or metaphors to make complex ideas or situations more relatable. Avoid generic references. For example, saying, *"She handed me a tattered, leather-bound journal with faded pages, filled with handwritten notes and pressed flowers"* is a lot more descriptive than, *"She handed me her journal."*

Incorporate examples that reflect common experiences or emotions that tap into shared human experiences. In doing so, your conversations will become more relatable and resonant.

For example, a statement like, *"I remember the feeling of butterflies in my stomach on the first day of school, the mix of excitement and nervousness all at once,"* reflects a common experience most everyone can relate to.

By incorporating descriptive details, examples and relatable experiences, you will increase the effectiveness of your communications.

Avoid Jargon

Using technical language or industry-specific jargon can be confusing for those who may not be familiar with it. It's always a safe bet to use clear and simple language to ensure your examples are easily understood by everyone. And, if you want to avoid sounding like a corporate robot, please refrain from using stale jargon like *"thinking outside the box."*

If you must use industry-specific terms or jargon that may be essential to your team's work, consider creating a shared document that defines and explains these terms for those who may not be as familiar with them as you may be. Using simple, clear language that is easy to understand is always a better approach.

Set an Expectation of Participation

Improv is a participation activity. In a similar vein, you must encourage participation from all team members in your business meetings. Just as in improv scenes, everyone has unique perspectives and ideas that foster innovation and creativity.

At the beginning of your meetings, make it clear that you encourage and expect everyone to participate and share their thoughts and ideas. Create a safe and supportive environment by making sure everyone feels comfortable and respected in the meeting. Encourage openness and a willingness to listen to all ideas! Use inclusive language that encourages all team members to participate.

> CREATE A SAFE AND SUPPORTIVE ENVIRONMENT BY MAKING SURE EVERYONE FEELS COMFORTABLE AND RESPECTED.

For example, instead of saying *"What do you think, Mike?"* say, *"What does everyone think?"*

Not only can you use the improv principle of, *"Yes, and..."* but also its sister principle, *"what if...?"* This involves asking "What if" questions to explore new possibilities, consider potential obstacles, and challenge conventional thinking.

This improv principle will assist teams in developing fresh ideas and approaches. When faced with a challenge, asking "What if" questions will help team members approach problems from different angles and identify potential solutions that they may not have considered otherwise.

For example, a team member may recommend a higher budget be allocated to social media advertising. A "what if" response could be, "Yes, and... what if we tap into the power of social media influencers who align with our values and target audience?"

Avoiding Assumptions

Often when we launch an improv scene, we assume our fellow players have an idea "where we're going with it." Sometimes they do, but many times they do not. We must be ready to veer from our intentions and meet them where *they* are. In a similar fashion, this happens with our team members, prospects, colleagues and clients.

When we make assumptions, we risk misunderstanding their

message and potentially damaging the communication. Never assume that you know what someone else is thinking or feeling. Instead, simply ask them to clarify their perspective. Ask open-ended questions that encourage discussion and invite diverse perspectives. This helps uncover different viewpoints and prevents assumptions based on limited information. Questions and clarifications will confirm your understanding. For example, questions like, *"Can you clarify what you mean by that?"* or *"Can you provide an example of your idea?"* to ensure you have correctly understood their message. Be inquisitive by cultivating a mindset of curiosity.

Be aware of your own biases and preconceived notions. Challenge your assumptions by considering alternative viewpoints and exploring different possibilities. This open-minded approach allows for more robust discussions and better decision-making. After meetings, take time to reflect on your assumptions and how they may have influenced your thinking or interactions. Learn from these experiences to continuously improve your communication skills and avoid making similar assumptions in the future!

Embracing Uncertainty

Embracing uncertainty is a fundamental principle of improv because it requires the improvisers to be spontaneous and flexible in response to unpredictable situations and circumstances in their scene work. They must be willing to take risks and embrace the unexpected!

Embracing uncertainty involves letting go of the need for control and instead, *accepting the reality that the scene can go in any direction.* Rather than trying to plan out every detail, improvisers must focus on listening and reacting to their scene partner's ideas, which creates a collaborative and dynamic performance. By accepting uncertainty, they can create engaging and unique scenes. It also helps to build trust and collaboration between performers; thus, they learn to rely on one another and support each other's ideas. By being open to the unexpected and trusting in their own abilities, improvisers create engaging performances!

Similarly, embracing uncertainty in business communication involves being comfortable with the unknown and adapting to unpredictable situations. This can be challenging because many people are accustomed to having control and structure in their work environment. However, embracing uncertainty can lead to improved problem-solving, increased innovation, and more effective decision-making.

EMBRACING UNCERTAINTY CAN LEAD TO IMPROVED PROBLEM-SOLVING, INCREASED INNOVATION, AND MORE EFFECTIVE DECISION-MAKING.

Develop a mindset that sees uncertainty as an opportunity for learning and growth rather than a threat. It seldom ever is.

Challenges and setbacks are chances to develop new skills, gain valuable insights, and discover innovative solutions. Be open to adjusting plans, strategies, and approaches based on new information or market conditions. Embrace flexibility and diverse perspectives through input from team members with varied backgrounds and expertise. These viewpoints will shed light on alternative solutions and identify opportunities in uncertain situations.

Embrace a mindset of *Kaizen*. Kaizen is a Japanese term that translates to "continuous improvement" or "change for better." It is a methodology focused on making incremental and continuous improvements in processes, products, and practices.

The core idea of Kaizen is to encourage small, gradual, and ongoing improvements rather than large-scale changes. It emphasizes the involvement of everyone, from top management to frontline workers, in identifying opportunities for improvement and implementing solutions. This approach aims to create a culture of constant improvement, where everyone is empowered to contribute to making processes more efficient, reducing waste, and enhancing overall quality.

Encourage experimentation and risk-taking within your team. Accept that some experiments may fail, but, again, view those failures as valuable learning experiences. Encourage employees to think creatively, challenge the status quo, and generate new ideas. That's improvising!

Focusing on What You Know

Don't be an "armchair quarterback." Armchair quarterbacking is a sports term and refers to the act of criticizing or offering advice on a situation or decision from the comfort of one's
armchair or without actually being directly involved or responsible for the outcome of the game. In other words, expressing opinions or making judgments about how a player,
coach, or team should have acted or performed during a
game. Armchair quarterbacking most always occurs after the
fact, when the outcome of a situation is already known, and
we then speculate on what could have been done differently
for a better result. However, this overlooks the complexities,
pressures, and constraints that the individuals directly involved may have faced at the time.

This can also happen during business meetings. To avoid
looking (or sounding) "stupid," one banters on about something they know little or nothing about. For those more aware
of the situation's details, this person's opinion is viewed with
less appreciation as they do not possess the benefit of
firsthand experience or a comprehensive understanding of the
situation.

It is important to consider the context, challenges, and limitations faced by those involved before offering judgments or advice. Put your ego away. Acknowledge any uncertainties up-
front and be transparent about what you know and what you
don't know. This can help you build trust with your audience,

prospects, clients or team members, making them more receptive to your message.

When you're unsure about something, use qualifiers like *"maybe," "probably,"* or *"possibly."* This can help you avoid making false statements and communicate your uncertainty more effectively. Instead of dwelling on what you don't know, focus on what you *do* know and communicate that clearly! Pretty simple, right?

Being Open to Shifts

Improv is organic. We start with an audience suggestion and build a scene surrounding that suggestion. We must be open to allowing it to blossom. In business communication, we must also be open to fluctuating plans or approaches. This assists us in adapting to new information, while making better decisions. If you're unsure about how your message is being received, ask for feedback! Use the magic question, *"What are your thoughts?"*

Uncertainty is a natural part of business, and, as it exists in improv, being able to embrace it will help you communicate more effectively while making better decisions. Rather than trying to control every aspect of a situation, simply focus on adapting to changes and finding creative solutions. Taking risks and trying new approaches requires a level of trust in yourself as well as your team members. It can be challenging, but it can also lead to increased innovation, better problem-solving, and more effective collaboration!

Humor? Maybe...

Humor can be a powerful tool in business communication, but it can also be risky to use effectively. Understanding who you're communicating with and what kind of humor might resonate with them is key to successfully using humor in a business setting. While humor can be a great way to build rapport, diffuse tension, and make a memorable impression, it's important to be tasteful. Avoid making jokes that are offensive or could be construed as inappropriate.

Humor works best in situations where the stakes are relatively low, so it's generally best to avoid it when the topic at hand is sensitive or emotionally charged. When incorporating humor into your communication, consider your audience. Humor that works for one audience might not work for another, so it's vitally important to tailor it to your audience.

Using self-deprecating humor is most always the safest humor. Self-deprecating humor is a form of humor in which one makes jokes or remarks that belittle or mock *ourselves*, often highlighting our own perceived flaws, mistakes, or shortcomings. It can be an effective way to connect with others, demonstrate humility, and create a lighthearted atmosphere. *"I'm an expert at finding the coffee machine, but when it comes to navigating the office building, I have a black belt in getting lost."*

It's important not to overdo this type of humor however, as

too much self-deprecation can come across as insincere or disingenuous. Tread lightly Grasshopper.

Humor is a skill like any other; the more you practice, the better you'll get at it. Look for opportunities to use humor in your day-to-day interactions, and pay attention to what works and what doesn't.

About Failure and Risks

In the world of improv, failure is viewed as a chance to learn and grow, rather than a cause for shame or embarrassment. Embracing mistakes as part of the learning process allows improv performers to learn and improve. Improv is a team effort, so encouraging and supporting fellow players is important, even when things don't go as planned. After our shows, we debrief and reflect on show scenes, discussing what worked well, what didn't, and how we can improve in the future. Encouraging performers to share their thoughts and ideas helps future performances and cultivates a culture of experimentation and growth.

Practice self-compassion. This is a psychological concept that involves treating yourself with the same kindness, understanding, and care that one would offer to a close friend in times of difficulty or suffering. Be mindful of your own challenges without judgment, and responding to yourself with empathy and self-kindness. Self-compassion is essential in embracing failure and taking risks. Improv performers cannot dwell on mistakes or failures but must quickly bounce back and move on to new ideas and opportunities. When things go well, they acknowledge the risks they took behind their successful scenes.

This mindset can be applied to business communications by encouraging team members to take risks and try new things without fear of failure or negative consequences. Accepting failures and taking risks are essential for innovation and growth in any business.

Unfortunately, failure is often seen negatively and best to be avoided. However, celebrating failure can be a powerful tool for fostering a culture of experimentation, risk-taking, and learning within a team. Team members must feel comfortable sharing their failures through open and honest communication. Reframing failure as an opportunity to learn and grow encourages risk-taking and experimentation.

When someone on the team shares a failure, it's important to celebrate the learning that emerged from it. Acknowledging the effort and courage it took to share the failure and highlighting the lessons learned!

Encouraging a growth mindset helps team members see failure as a chance to improve rather than a reflection of their abilities. Celebrating efforts, even when they don't go as planned, fosters a culture of openness where team members feel empowered to take risks and try new things.

If you are a leader, you must make a strong effort to model the behavior you want to see in your team. Team members must recognize they have permission to fail. Provide support to those who have taken risks or experienced failure. Share your experiences with your team to inspire them to do the same. Encourage them to share their ideas and opinions, and be open to trying new approaches. Even if an idea doesn't work out, it's important to *celebrate the effort* and encourage continued experimentation!

Share the Spotlight

Face it, most all of us love attention. Sometimes our selfish egos kick-in, and we turn into competitive little kids, trying to get the audience's attention. However, as improv performers, we must be present in the moment... *without* grandstanding and attempting to hog the scene.

Instead, we must embrace the fine art of making our improv partners look good on stage. No, I'm not talking about straightening their collars or adjusting their hairstyle, I'm talking about giving up the spotlight to them when carrying out a scene.

Before every improv show, the green room is buzzing with team players patting each of their teammates on the back, making eye contact and saying, "got your back." This is done not only out of tradition, but also the recognition of creating a show out of nothing in front of strangers can sometime be a frightening experience, and that we are supportive of our fellow players.

Our scene partners are our collaborators and they actively support us, as we must do in supporting them. Without respecting and supporting our fellow players, we would be reduced to a boring monologue. It's all about having their back, exercising a team effort destined for an enjoyable scene. We must shed our egos!

This same ego wants to shine brightly in our communication efforts. We must release our ego and make ourselves vulnerable. The conversation or meeting isn't about you; *it's about the totality of the circumstances you are merely participating in.*

At times, this may mean you have to "take a backseat." There's nothing the matter with that. Have you ever seen Johnny Carson interview Rodney Dangerfield on *The Tonight Show?* Johnny continually fed Rodney lead-ins for his famous "no respect" branding, using questions like *"How's your wife and kids?"* or *"How's your health?"* Rodney then rolled out his standard jokes. He got the laughs and Carson got the ratings. A win-win.

Again, you must think about what you can contribute to the conversation rather than what you can take from it. Everyone's goal should be to set up their fellow team members for success.

When we can trust that our team members and fellow staffers "have our back," we feel safe to be courageous and contribute.

We feel comfortable in getting out of our head and pouring our creative thoughts into the challenge at hand.

The more diligent we are in setting up others for success, the better opportunity we have of effectively accomplishing our team's overall mission. When we're more focused on "our own stuff," it costs our team members time and energy, damages our momentum and sometimes injures our reputation.

Set your team members up for a win. Replace any thoughts of competition with thoughts of cooperation. *Cooperate with others; compete with yourself.* Make it your mission to create pathways of success for those you lead. Make a habit of reminding the people in your life that you "got their back!"

Non-verbal communication tools are essential tools for improv performers. It assists us in connecting with our scene partners using body language and facial expressions. Non-verbal communication makes scenes more realistic and engaging for the audience.

Improvisers make sure their physicality (movements and postures) match the demeanor and emotions their character is portraying.

This same nonverbal communication skill can also play an important role in business meetings, as it assists in reinforcing your message while establishing valuable rapport with your team members. Let's take a look at some tips for using nonverbal communication effectively during business meetings...

Put their NEED before
your GREED.

— Joe Hammer

Chapter 6

Harnessing Nonverbal Communication Secrets

The Unconscious Communication Tools

Non-verbal communication tools are essential tools for improv performers. It assists us in connecting with our scene partners using body language and facial expressions. Nonverbal communication makes scenes more realistic and engaging for the audience.

Improvisers make sure their physicality (movements and postures) match the demeanor and emotions their character is portraying. Facial expressions convey and communicate the character's emotions a range of emotions. Surprise. Anger. Happiness. Jealousy.

This same nonverbal communication skill can also play an important role in business meetings, as it assists in reinforcing your message while establishing valuable rapport with your team members. Unlock the power of nonverbal communication in your business meetings with these impactful tips:

Eye Contact

In improv, making eye contact serves as a crucial tool for building a connection with our scene partners. It's a visible sign that everyone is fully engaged, actively listening, and responding to each other. If you've ever watched an improv performance, you may have noticed that one performer can simply lock eyes with another to invite them into a scene. It's akin to a form of unspoken, almost psychic, communication!

Confidence. Attentiveness. Respect. Establishing and maintaining eye contact with your team members can help to convey these during a brainstorming session or team meeting. Maintaining eye contact establishes trust, demonstrates attentiveness, and conveys respect.

When in a conversation with someone, focus on their eyes. Doing so will help you to stay engaged and attentive, while conveying a sense of respect and interest. Avoid staring though as it can often make others feel uncomfortable. Maintain a natural and relaxed gaze. Periodically take breaks from eye contact. It's also a great time to gather your thoughts.

Facial Expressions

Facial expressions convey engagement and interest. Use them! They powerfully emphasize key points you're making during a meeting. A smile or nod can effectively demonstrate agreement. They're a nonverbal "Yes, and......!"

Raising your eyebrows slightly will indicate that you're attentively listening, while furrowing them can demonstrate a concern or disagreement. Leaning forward and nodding demonstrates you're engaged and interested. Be sure to smile, as it's
a valuable tool to help put others at ease while conveying a
friendly and approachable demeanor. Don't overdo it however, as a constant smile can come across as disingenuous as a
shady used car salesman.

Couple your expressions to the message you desire to convey.
If you're discussing a serious issue, your expressions should
reflect the seriousness of the situation. If you're conveying enthusiasm for a project, your expressions must be upbeat and
energetic.

If you're not sure how your facial expressions come across,
practice in front of a mirror. This is a common practice among
successful improvisers! Begin by practicing basic facial expressions such as smiling, nodding, and making eye contact.
Then practice making emotional expressions such as surprise,
curiosity, or concern. Pay attention to subtle changes in your
facial expressions, such as slight eyebrow movements or
changes in your mouth shape.

Your trusty mirror can help you develop a wider range of nonverbal communication and become more comfortable expressing a variety of emotions. Expressions will help convey
confidence and positivity during a meeting. They will also
help you become more aware of your nonverbal cues and how
they may be perceived by others!

Banish Distractions

Finally, it's important to avoid distractions that can interfere with your ability to connect. Distractions can seriously impact our ability to focus and be productive.

Yes, put away your phone. Don't use it to take notes. Go the old-fashioned route of using the tried-and-true pen and paper.

Practice Mindfulness

Mindfulness is simply the practice of being fully present and engaged in the moment. Doing so will keep you focused. To effectively use mindfulness during a meeting, prepare yourself before the discussion by taking a few deep breaths and focusing your mind on the present moment and topic at hand. Stay present. Remain engaged in the discussion.

If your mind begins to wander (and it will...), gently bring your attention back to the present moment. Avoid criticism of yourself or others. Show compassion to others who may be feeling overwhelmed, stressed or disconnected from the meeting topic. This will create a more positive atmosphere and encourage more creative conversations.

Sometimes meetings go a bit long. When that happens, take a break and allow everyone a little stretch time. When returning, resume the meeting with a quick improv warm-up to re-energize (See Bonus Section). It will improve everyone's focus and energize the remainder of the meeting.

Body Language

Were you aware that your body language often conveys more than your spoken words? Indeed, it does. Your posture, gestures, and movements reveal more than you might recognize. Leaning forward, for example, signifies genuine engagement in the conversation, whereas crossing your arms sends a clear message of skepticism or unwillingness to be persuaded.

Effective communication relies heavily on body language; however, we often unintentionally display negative body language without realizing it. Avoid fidgeting or making unnecessary movements, as this can be distracting and take away from your message.

Mirroring of another's body language is a powerful tool for communication. During my studies of Neuro-Linguistic Programming (NLP), mirroring was emphasized as an important technique. Mirroring is the art of becoming a human chameleon!

When two people mirror each other's body language, it can create a sense of mutual understanding and trust, leading to better communication and a more positive interaction. For example, if someone leans forward and nods during a conversation, the other person mirrors this behavior by also leaning forward and nodding. Just be sure your mirroring isn't distracting or "over-the-top" as it can come across as insincere or manipulative. In other words, just don't be too obvious with your mirroring efforts. Gently mimic their posture, gestures, and facial expressions.

Don't be afraid to throw in some gestures. As an Italian, it comes naturally to me! Suitable gestures will help emphasize your point while making your message more impactful.

Mirroring can be used strategically to build rapport with clients or colleagues, negotiate better deals, and improve teamwork. It's secret way to build a connection with others without them even realizing it. Pretty sneaky, right? But hey, it works!

Tonality

Your tone of voice is like a secret agent that sneaks around, conveying emotions and attitudes without you even knowing it! However, you must be careful how you use it as your message might end up lost in translation. Check in with yourself to see how you're feeling before communicating. If you're feeling stressed or frustrated, your tone of voice could come across harsh or critical. Also pay attention to the other's tone of voice. This can help you better understand their perspectives.

Make sure you are speaking clearly and at a volume that is appropriate for the setting. Avoid speaking too loudly or too softly. Use a friendly tone, even if you are discussing a difficult topic or giving constructive feedback. This will put others at ease, making them more receptive to your message.

Being aware of and practicing your nonverbal communication skills, you can enhance your message, build rapport with your team members, and create a more collaborative and productive meeting environment.

Growth comes when you challenge the personal opinions you have about yourself.

— Joe Hammer

Chapter 7

Connecting With Your Audience

Tell Me a Story

Storytelling in improv is like baking a cake. You need the right ingredients. Things like engaging character personalities, stimulating dialog and interesting themes. Storytelling assists improvisers in creating engaging and memorable scenes. Timing is also an important element. Performers need to know when to add new information to the scene and when to hold back. In doing so they create a sense of tension or suspense that keeps the audience engaged. This requires a strong sense of pacing and a learned ability to read the scene dynamics and adjust accordingly.

In the business environment, make sure the story you choose is relevant to the topic of discussion and will resonate with your audience. Storytelling will humanize your message. Use stories to illustrate key points and to clarify complex concepts. Stories will also make your point more memorable than mere "facts and figures."

Use emotions to engage your team members to evoke an emotive response. In doing so it is more likely to be remembered and acted upon. Use vivid and descriptive language to help your team members visualize the details, making it more engaging and memorable. Avoid adding unneeded details that could detract from the message.

Descriptive Language

In improv, we say, "Show, don't tell." Instead of simply telling your team members what you desire to achieve, show them with descriptive stories. Your story will come alive by using vivid and expressive language. Create a picture in your team members' minds. Use stories to illustrate how the vision will look and feel. Use personal anecdotes to show them how the vision connects to their own experiences and goals. They must see themselves as part of the vision!

Characters

Effective improv players always have a variety of characters in their repertoire. Characters are the heart of any story, so improv performers must be able to create characters that are interesting and engaging. Although we don't associate the importance of character development in the business world, it does indeed play a vital role. How? They help to bring your message to life by making it more relatable to your audience. When assembling a story to make a point, interject a character's personality to best represent the perspective or point of view you desire.

If you are talking about a past client, prospective customer, vendor or competitor, give them a unique personality! Characters are the salt and pepper of business communication as they spice up even the most boring and bland ideas. Give complex concepts a fun and relatable character to explain them and it has the power to turn a snooze-fest into a party that everyone wants to attend!

Personal Anecdotes

Sharing a personal story can assist in building a strong connection with your team. It can also help illustrate your points in a heart-centered, relatable way. Just be authentic. Don't attempt to "force" a personal story if it doesn't feel natural. Be honest and genuine when sharing your experiences. Keep it succinct; short and to the point. Avoid using jargon or technical language that may be confusing. Remember that you're not just telling a story but instead, illustrating a point.

The Value

Choose a story that resonates and aligns with your desired goal or outcome; one that captures attention and everyone can relate to. Share stories about how the impact of your product or service has had on its marketplace. Use specific examples as they will help everyone better understand the impact of the point you desire to make. Use anecdotes and stories of individuals whose lives have been positively impacted by your company's product, service or process.

The Call to Action

End your story with a *Call to Action*. What's the point? What do you desire your team to do with the information you've provided in the story? What can they do to achieve the outcome that's desired? What has inspired them to take action?

A well-crafted call to action is :

Clear: It should leave no ambiguity about what action is expected from your audience.

Actionable: It should be something the audience can realistically do.

Motivating: It should be compelling and persuasive, appealing to the audience's emotions, needs, or desires.

Timely: It should convey a sense of urgency if applicable.

Measurable: In some cases, it's important to have a way to track and measure the response to the CTA.

The effectiveness of a presentation often hinges on the strength and relevance of its call to action. Whether it's closing a sale, inspiring change, or fostering engagement, it can powerfully drive desired outcomes.

Chapter 8

Overcoming Fear and Uncertainty

Mistakes as Opportunities

In the unpredictable world of improv, mistakes come with the territory! Given its spontaneous nature, mistakes do happen... and quite often. The key is getting past them and moving forward to a logical (and hopefully humorous) conclusion.

Improv requires *decisiveness*, as players must utter the first thing that comes to their mind, even though the result of their decision is sometimes a bit obscure. They rely on their scene partners to "have their back" and assist by agreeing with their statement and adding a response to move the scene forward. Yep, it's "Yes, and...!..."

We often waste time by over-analyzing. In improv and in life, we must learn to just make a decision, and move on. Sure, in life it requires a bit more thought than a simple improv scene, but the concept is the same; *move things forward.*

In our youth improv classes, I routinely incorporate games that are specifically designed to turn failure into a source of outrageous enjoyment. These exercises, which focus on building confidence, consistently stand out as the favorites. As soon as the participants grasp the concept that there's no way to do it "incorrectly," and that errors are integral to the enjoyment, they undergo a remarkable transformation in terms of personal expression and creativity.

Failure is just a sign that we're learning faster than a kid on a sugar high. Don't sweat the small stuff and embrace the oopsies, because that's where real learning and breakthroughs happen!

Think about it; many great inventions were either based on or resulted from mistakes. As Edison worked on perfecting his light bulb invention, he didn't dwell on his numerous setbacks. Instead, he regarded them as unproven hypotheses. He willingly faced the potential of disappointing his peers and never entertained the notion that his invention might ultimately fail.

The Post-It Note® was a failed attempt by chemists at 3M. It was the *accidental discovery and recognition of the product's potential* that led to the creation of this simple yet revolutionary product that has had a significant impact on how we communicate and organize information.

New improvisers always make mistakes. However, we are trained to respond to these mistakes as "gifts," The same is true in life, the boardroom, or with your sales team at the office. Mistakes are stepping stones to growth.

In the past, mistakes frequently led to us being reprimanded in front of our peers at school. Likewise, a low exam score would bring negative repercussions on our report cards. Strangely enough, the fear of making mistakes has transformed into our current reality. These life situations have established a mental pattern that we feel compelled to evade. Our inner dialogue adds to the problem with self-criticism, deepening the fear conditioning through self-inflicted negativity: *"Others will think I'm stupid."*

We were taught the importance of seeking and arriving at that one "right" answer. We've become blunder phobic – fearing our mistakes are going to make us appear that we're less than we desire to be. Then we move on to our careers – where mistakes are frowned upon – many times to the point of letting down our fellow team members, demotion or even losing our job.

> **WE'VE BECOME BLUNDER PHOBIC – FEARING OUR MISTAKES ARE GOING TO MAKE US APPEAR THAT WE'RE LESS THAN WE DESIRE TO BE.**

Pulling from hundreds of negative events from our subconsciously-stored historic recordings, our mind's power to self-assault is merciless! Our anxiety rises even when we *think* of making a mistake! As these mistake-centered events occur in our lives, we eventually begin developing strategies to avoid making them - everything from becoming a perfectionist to simply being afraid of attempting anything outside of our comfort zone.

What we fail to realize is that mistakes are gifts of growth, for, without them, we would never achieve any new accomplishments in our life.

Many people are caught up with what I call, *"The Passion of Perfection."* This goes beyond mere perfectionism; it entails becoming immobilized by the fear that whatever we do won't meet the standard. It's the point at which we fail to take action due to our internal pessimistic self-talk, self-critique, and the dread of making a mistake.

People experiencing this problem are aware of it but many times can't seem to shake it. They start a myriad of self-incriminating questions, like, *"should I do [insert action plan #1] or [insert action plan #2]?"*

Then they'll go on to unearth often fictitious problems, challenges and difficulties related to *both* of their possible choices. The result? Inaction and staying with the status quo. And with that my friend, there is no growth.

Failing really isn't the colossal setback our minds have made it up to be. *It's the lack of training in techniques to move forward after failing that holds us back.* Everyone screws up, but if you demonstrate that a mistake doesn't define you, and you demonstrate the capability of moving forward, then others will follow your lead and move forward as well!

Mistakes are an inevitable part of life. On the bright side, they play a crucial role by fostering growth, prompting us to reconsider our approach, and guiding us toward adjusted actions to achieve our intended outcomes. Think of it like an aircraft operating on autopilot – it continuously makes course adjustments to ensure it reaches its destination.

I've seen major blunders in improv shows, situations where one player is not paying attention to what their fellow player is saying or doing. For example, let's assume the audience gives a one-word suggestion for the scene... the word *"monkey."* Immediately and without any forethought, players enter as monkeys. Outside of screeching, grunting and picking bugs from each other's hair, once these players landed on this response, there's nowhere else to go. Their unsophisticated thinking and premature decision left them little room to improvise.

Experienced improvisers would avoid resorting to an overtly predictable response to the scene. Perhaps one player can set the scene as an "accelerated evolution" story. In doing so, they narrate the process of evolving from primate to human. The other player picks up on the direction, accepts this reality and follows along, demonstrating their fellow player's story, initially speaking in caveman grunts, perhaps even ending "the evolution" as a boastful politician!

Alternatively, the initial scene could entail one player as a senior staff member at the zoo, assisting the other player on their first day on the job at the monkey exhibit. Or possibly a monkey-handler, who is attempting to place a spider-monkey on the shoulder of a zoo visitor with a deeply-rooted fear of primates.

By players consciously *discounting the obvious* when the topic is announced, creativity will come into play for a much more enticing and engaging scene. This requires thinking on a different, often deeper level.

Again, mistakes are gifts; doorways to a new adventure. This perceived "mistake" of players choosing to be monkeys can be converted into an enjoyable and funny scene if the players are conscious of the error and commit to the progression of the scene.

The obvious choice is seldom the best choice. Improv, just as in business communication, is all about *accepting and building.*

Just like in many of life's challenges, there are multiple paths to choose from, and there isn't always a single correct answer. Conversely, there are individuals who seem to be indifferent to making mistakes, which is more of a lazy approach and isn't sustainable, whether it's in the realm of improv or business communication. I remember having an employee like that in the past. When confronted with a mistake that was clearly preventable, his response was simply, "Nobody's perfect."

Sure, that's a very true statement; however, when simple mistakes are continually made because of one's failure to recognize the consequences of their actions, then it's a different story.

I once asked him, *"Mark, how many babies do you think they drop in the delivery room?"*

He looked at me puzzled, *"None,"* he said awkwardly.

"That's correct," I replied, *"the reason is that they realize the severity and consequences of their mistakes. Sure, nobody's perfect, but they are trained to take precautions to avoid the problem before it occurs. You must do the same thing."*

He agreed, and his frequent errors in judgement were soon greatly reduced.

Don't strive to live in an imaginary world of perfection; however, don't foolishly act without a bit of defined thought. Take a beat before taking action. Pause. When a mistake occurs, avoid self-punishment and blame, make adjustments, and move forward.

Improv scenes are born from players' innovative imaginations, but as I often say to my students, *"If you dig a hole, I'm not saving you."*

For example, if you start the scene by establishing your partner as a serpent-like space alien that eats only eggshells and lives in tunnels under Disneyland, then you're responsible for *owning up to all those details.* It won't be easy, and you'll quickly discover the result of your pointless attempt at being funny will backfire... What you've made difficult for your scene partner has now become just as difficult for you as well.

In business communications, we do a similar thing by going off on too many tangents, causing our team members to forget the original point!

Heed the advice of your parents when they told you to treat

others the way you desired to be treated. Always set up your team members for success.

Remember, *mistakes are gifts; don't fear making them.* Respond to them without negative self-criticism. Find the opportunities hidden within them. Transform and redirect them into a positive life experience. Celebrate them!

Improv as well as effective communication are both collaborative art forms that rely on trust and support. Taking risks opens your team to discovery of new ideas and approaches. Without embracing risks, they may never push themselves beyond their comfort zones and explore their full range of their creativity. Celebrate mistakes as opportunities for learning and growth as well as an essential part of creativity!

For every mistake that you learn from you will save thousands of similar mistakes in the future, so if you treat mistakes as learning opportunities that yield rapid improvements you should be excited by them. But if you treat them as bad things, you will make yourself and others miserable, and you won't grow.

Chapter 9

Improv to Strengthen Team Relationships

Trust is a necessary component of successful improv performance. On stage, we all must trust our fellow players to listen, support, and collaborate with us.

Many progressive organization and management programs have harnessed the power of improv techniques to teach creativity, collaboration and co-creating. The results have proven it can energize teams, surface breakthrough ideas, and enable learning from failure.

In my corporate training program, *Influential Interactions,* I use Principles of Improv to help company staff members and leaders transform their management and communication approach in their daily interactions. Participants uncover a distinct and unconventional focus that alters how their brain processes and shares information.

More Than One Right Answer

There's always more than one right answer to any given dilemma. One of my favorite business development books is *A Whack on the Side of the Head* by Roger Von Oech.

He says,

> *"By the time the average person finishes college, he or she will have taken over 2,600 tests, quizzes, and exams. The right answer approach becomes deeply ingrained in our thinking. This may be fine for some mathematical problems where there is in fact only one right answer. The difficulty is that most of life isn't this way. Life is ambiguous; there are many right answers - all depending on what you're looking for. But if you think there is only one right answer, then you'll stop looking as soon as you find one."*

When an improv scene begins, many elements come into play. It's raw. Unfocused. Non-specific. A "right" answer (approach) doesn't exist. As it plays out, the focus eventually gets more distinct. No player is in charge or in control. Improv is a very organic and ever-changing environment. A player may have a set idea of where a story "should" go, but they quickly have to discard that idea as soon as they hear what their fellow player has to say, which many times is in a different direction. The improv player is never panic-stricken because they know that their fellow players have their back.

Similarly, when engaged in team conversations about direction, strategy or creativity, team members often feel they have to select *one* idea to run with. Many times, they decide on that idea too early, thus missing many other more creative solutions.

When given an assignment to resolve a company challenge, a successful team requires harmony and cohesion between the team members. Improv assists in this interpersonal communication skill. The process becomes more organic, many times leading to a result that otherwise would have been overlooked by using conventional team efforts. Team building with elements of improvisation makes the process more about *collaboration,* not *competition.*

Improv players know the importance of making their fellow players look good, and the same holds true with an effective project team. The better they make their partners look, the better the result will be. I can always tell how much experience one has in improv when they enter the stage with "some really great idea" about their character or scene idea in their head. The problem is, their fellow players likely have absolutely no idea what's brewing in their eager mind. No matter how brilliant an idea might be, it's worthless if the entire scene goes bad.

The same principle applies to communication in meetings. If individuals are solely focused on their own perspectives and not open to input from their team members, the final result will likely be less successful.

Team Narratives

Old school thinking proposes that an effective team leader must communicate to everyone what they must do. However, today's team leader looks to the future, is innovative, and recognizes that their job is to ask the right questions while providing their team with nominal structure and true independence. If someone makes a mistake, everyone needs to jump in and take care of it. Noble work gets accomplished when everyone has each other's back and looks out for the best interest of their teammates.

Effective leaders have enormous advantages when they listen and engage in open dialogue with their staff or team members. We cannot attain alignment, empowerment or accountability without enthusiastically engaging our crew. Leaders must be open and accepting, even if they initially disagree.

LEADERS MUST BE OPEN AND ACCEPTING, EVEN IF THEY INITIALLY DISAGREE.

By applying the principles of improv, you and your team members will swiftly cultivate a sense of pride and co-create an enjoyable narrative. The improv mindset will aid in uncovering distinctive solutions to the challenges your team encounters.

Non-Conventional Uses of Improv

Improv techniques can be applied to most all communication environments! Using them, you can strengthen relationships and build trust effortlessly. Here are some examples of improv's "unconventional" uses:

Improv in Marriage Counseling

A couple was having communication issues, and traditional talk therapy wasn't helping. They decided to try something different and worked with a therapist who incorporated improv exercises into their sessions. Through improv exercises, the couple was able to improve their communication skills, build trust, and become more playful with each other. As a result, their relationship improved, and they reported feeling more connected and satisfied with their marriage.

Improv in Team Building

A team at a tech startup company was struggling with collaboration and communication. They decided to try an improv workshop as a team-building exercise. Using improv techniques, the team was able to break down barriers and work more collaboratively. They learned to actively listen to each other, build on each other's ideas, and trust each other's instincts. As a result, the team's productivity and morale improved, and they reported feeling more connected as a group.

Improv in Family Therapy

A family was having difficulty communicating and resolving conflicts. They worked with a therapist who incorporated improv exercises into their sessions. In doing so, the family members were able to better understand each other's perspectives, practice active listening, and build trust. They learned to be more playful with each other, which helped reduce tension and improve their relationships. As a result, the family reported feeling closer and more connected.

Improv in Sales

A sales team was struggling to connect with potential clients during pitches. They decided to incorporate improv exercises into their training sessions to improve their communication skills. Soon the sales team became more confident in their communication and build trust with potential clients. They learned to actively listen to their clients, respond to their needs, and adapt their pitches to each client's unique situation. As a result, the sales team was able to build stronger relationships with their clients and increase their sales.

Improv in Crisis Communication

A company was facing a public relations crisis and needed to communicate with stakeholders in a clear and effective way. They worked with a crisis communication consultant who incorporated improv exercises into their training sessions. Through the practice of improv, the company's spokesperson became more confident in their communication, actively listen to stakeholders, and respond to their needs. The spokesperson was also able to build trust by showing empathy and transparency, which helped to rebuild the company's reputation.

These examples offer a glimpse into how the principles of improv can be utilized in a variety of fields in fostering trust and enhancing collaboration. Now, there's no reason not to apply them in your own communication environments!

Chapter 10

Improv in Meetings and Brainstorming Sessions

As I've emphasized, improv is undeniably a "team sport." When players step onto the stage, their main responsibility is to make their fellow players shine. Successful business communications operate on the same principle—it's not about your individual recognition, but instead about what each person brings to the table and acceptance of others' contributions.

Goals and Objectives

While improv principles are often associated with creativity and spontaneity, they can also be applied to setting clear goals and objectives. As I've mentioned, improv scenes start with a "suggestion" from the audience. If they say, *"A newlywed couple on their honeymoon night in a haunted hotel,"* that's our goal as well as objective – to play this scenario out to a logical and humorous ending.

Although your business meeting may not be as exciting as a haunted honeymoon, it is still essential to set clear objectives for your team so that everyone knows what they are working towards. Doing so helps to keep everyone focused and motivated.

Again, embrace the "Yes, and..." mindset as we discussed in Chapter 3. Instead of rejecting ideas, embrace and build upon them to develop clear and achievable goals. Be open to new ideas. As improv players, we must be open and ready to respond to whatever ideas and directions become present in the scene. The same is true in business communication. When setting goals, be willing to explore new ideas and approaches to achieve them.

Improv players always maintain focus on the present moment, responding to what unfolds in that moment. Similarly, when establishing goals, it's important to concentrate on what can be achieved in the present, rather than dwelling on the past or anticipating future obstacles. Collaboration is vital in improv, as it enables players to create a cohesive performance. Likewise, fostering collaboration among team members is key to developing shared objectives.

Nurture a Positive Environment

Creating a positive work environment holds considerable influence over both productivity and creativity. Similarly, in the context of an improv performance, fellow players offer high-fives along with the reassuring phrase, "got your back." This practice embodies their commitment to supporting each other's success during the performance. They actively ensure that their teammates don't face situations that might make them appear less competent and collaborate to establish a secure and encouraging space where everyone is at ease contributing to the scenes.

Likewise, your team members must feel comfortable sharing their thoughts and opinions without fear of criticism or ridicule. This is done by encouraging open communication, respect, and collaboration. Building on each other's ideas in a positive environment will make team members feel heard and valued.

Improv requires playfulness and spontaneity. Encourage team members to approach work with a similar sense of playfulness. Who says business can't be fun? Look at some of the most progressive companies and you'll discover playfulness to be an integral element of their collaboration process! *Google. Zappos. Airbnb.* Employees of these companies often use games, activities, and other creative exercises to brainstorm, solve problems, and build relationships. Allow your team to approach challenges with creativity and enthusiasm!

Feedback

As we all know, feedback is important in growth and effective communication. Feedback helps everyone understand their strengths as well as areas needing improvement. As improv players, we celebrate both our successes and failures as a way to learn and grow our art. Our failures are often funnier (and better learning tools) than our successes!

OUR FAILURES ARE OFTEN FUNNIER (AND BETTER LEARNING TOOLS) THAN OUR SUCCESSES!

Be specific when providing feedback. Focus on the *action* or *process*, rather than the *person*. Encourage dialogue and collaboration when providing feedback. Ask questions to understand the team member's perspective and work together to develop solutions to any issues.

As improvisers, we constantly strive to improve our improv skills while developing new ones. Encourage the same mindset in the workplace by focusing on growth and development while providing needed feedback. Provide actionable steps for the team member to improve their work, rather than simply criticizing them.

End constructive feedback on a positive note by highlighting something the team member did well or expressing confidence in their ability to improve.

Collaboration is vital in improv, as it enables players to create a cohesive performance. Likewise, fostering collaboration among team members is key to developing shared objectives.

Chapter 11

Improv for Conflict Resolution and Negotiation

Better Communication

Progressive companies are using the dynamic principles of improv to enhance their staff's communication, negotiation, and conflict resolution skills. I have trained hundreds of business professionals in many industries to better communicate using the magic of improv principles. Here are some of the companies using improv communication techniques in their organizations:

Google

Google has used improv training to help its employees develop better communication and negotiation skills. The company's "Improvisational Leadership" program teaches employees to listen actively, collaborate effectively, and respond flexibly to changing situations.

Procter & Gamble

P&G has used improv training to help its employees develop better conflict resolution skills. The company's "Improvisational Dialogue" program teaches employees to listen actively, find common ground, and generate creative solutions to problems.

IBM

IBM has used improv training to help its sales team negotiate more effectively. The company's "Improvisational Selling" program teaches salespeople to listen actively, ask open-ended questions, and build rapport with clients.

Deloitte

Deloitte has used improv training to help its employees develop better communication and problem-solving skills. The company's "Improv for Business" program teaches employees to think creatively, work collaboratively, and respond flexibly to changing situations.

Microsoft

Microsoft has used improv training to help its employees develop better leadership and communication skills. The company's "Leadership Presence" program teaches employees to communicate effectively, build trust with others, and respond flexibly to challenges.

Zappos

This online shoe retailer has embraced the principles of improv. They encourage employees to take risks and experiment with new ideas, and incorporate improv exercises into their training programs. Zappos has found that improv helps to build confidence, improve communication, and foster a positive and supportive work culture.

Pixar

The animation studio Pixar utilizes improv as a way to foster creativity and collaboration. They have incorporated improv exercises into their brainstorming and ideation processes, encouraging employees to experiment and take risks. Pixar has found that improv helps to build a culture of trust and collaboration, which is essential in their highly collaborative work environment.

Southwest Airlines

This airline is known for its fun and upbeat company culture, which is built on principles of improv. Southwest encourages its employees to be creative and fosters an environment of collaboration and experimentation. They also use improv techniques to train employees in customer service and conflict resolution, helping them to think on their feet and build stronger relationships with passengers.

The Ritz-Carlton

The luxury hotel chain is known for its exceptional customer service, which is built on principles of improv. Ritz-Carlton employees are trained to listen actively, build on ideas, and provide personalized service to each guest. They also use improv techniques to train employees in problem-solving and conflict resolution, helping them to think on their feet and provide creative solutions to challenges.

Conciliation and Problem Solving

Improv techniques can also be an effective tool in resolving conflicts and better managing difficult conversations.

In the late 1990s, Apple Computer was in a difficult situation with one of its suppliers, Power Computing. Power Computing was producing clones of Apple's Macintosh computers, which threatened Apple's business. Apple's CEO, Steve Jobs, decided to use the "Yes, and..."principle of improv to negotiate with Power Computing's CEO. Instead of rejecting their proposal outright, Jobs listened to their concerns and built on their ideas, ultimately leading to a successful resolution of the conflict.

In 2017, United Airlines was embroiled in a public relations crisis when a passenger was forcibly removed from a flight. In the aftermath of the incident, United CEO Oscar Munoz used the improv technique, "Active Listening" to respond to customers' concerns and begin rebuilding trust. Munoz listened carefully to customers' feedback and used their input to make changes to United's policies and procedures.

Chapter 12

Improv for Presentations and Public Speaking

Improv principles can serve as powerful tools for enhancing your presentation and public speaking skills. They become particularly valuable when unexpected changes or unusual questions/comments arise from the audience. I've personally encountered situations where I was originally slated to deliver a 90-minute presentation, only to find out upon arrival that the meeting planner had to reduce it to 45 minutes due to modified event activities.

When giving a presentation, focus on the present moment rather than worrying about what comes next. Set up your presentation in a modular fashion, segmenting the information into bite-size bits of information. If your presentation time is as planned, you can expound more on the topics. Should the time be cut, due to your "modular" set up, you'll be ready with a down-sized, core version of the information.

Improv requires us to let go of any distracting thoughts or worries that may be pulling us out of the moment. We cannot be present if our minds are wondering or "thinking ahead." Practice mindfulness by being fully present. Connect with your audience. Look them in the eye and speak directly to them as if each one is the only one you are speaking to. This will assist in your feeling more grounded and present in the moment.

If you find yourself getting distracted, refocus your attention on your breath and your audience. Don't worry about being perfect (trust me, there is no such thing) or getting things to go exactly as planned. Allow yourself to be spontaneous and authentic in your presentation. That's improv!

Spontaneity and Adaptability

If there are two words that best describe improv, *spontaneity* and *adaptability* would be my choices. Improv requires players to respond to unexpected situations in the moment. You will soon discover that being spontaneous and adaptable in your presentations can make them more engaging and dynamic. You will be prepared for unexpected questions or interruptions, and ready to adapt your presentation as needed.

While it may seem counterintuitive, being adequately prepared will actually make you more spontaneous! When you're well-prepared, you're more confident in your content and can be more flexible in delivering that content!

Humor, Wit and Charm

Although you shouldn't come across as a comedian, incorporating humor into your presentation can make you more relatable and likable to your audience. Perhaps open your presentation with a joke or a lighthearted anecdote that relates to your topic. This can help to break the ice and set a playful tone for the rest of your presentation. It can also make your presentation appear more spontaneous and engaging. However, remember that humor is subjective. What one person may find funny, another might not.

As I've previously mentioned, before using humor, consider your audience and make sure your jokes or anecdotes are appropriate and relatable to them. Avoid controversial or offensive humor, and keep your jokes and anecdotes light and playful. Again, it's often best to use self-deprecating humor. It can be a great way to break the ice and build rapport with your audience. Don't overdo it, however. Use humor strategically to keep your audience engaged, but never make it the sole focus of your presentation.

Don't be fearful of mistakes or going "off-script." You shouldn't have a script to start with! All that's necessary is a list of topics and points relating to or supporting the topic. Avoid the old school "outline." The best moments in a presen-

> AVOID THE OLD SCHOOL "OUTLINE." THE BEST MOMENTS IN A PRESENTATION OFTEN OCCUR FROM UNEXPECTED SITUATIONS!

tation often occur from unexpected situations! Using the improv principles in this book and (as well as my other instrumental book, *The Improv Edge*) will assist you in effectively responding to unexpected situations. In doing so you will become more adaptable and engaging as a speaker.

Just like my improv students, practice improvisation to improve your ability to think on your feet and be spontaneous. Try incorporating some improv games in this book and *The Improv Edge* into your public speaking practice to help you develop this skill!

Visuals

Although you should never rely on PowerPoint to deliver your presentation, incorporating visuals and props that are relevant to your topic can add a bit of energy. They should complement and support your presentation, not "be" the presentation. From infographics to convey complex information to images and videos, these appeal to the visual folks in your audience.

You can also use physical props that are relevant to your presentation to help illustrate your points. For example, Zig Ziglar used an old-fashioned well-pump in his keynote to illustrate the importance

Zig Ziglar

of "priming the pump" in sales. He explained that when you first start pumping water from a well, it can be difficult to get the water flowing. You have to put in a lot of effort to get the water to start flowing, but once it starts flowing, it gets easier. He encouraged his audience to "prime the pump" by taking small steps towards their goals.

The key to using visual props effectively is to make sure they are relevant to your message and enhance your presentation, rather than detract from it. Use them sparingly and strategically, and always make sure they add value to your presentation.

The Key Phrase

Repetition can be a powerful tool when used effectively in public speaking. When introducing key concepts or ideas, use repetition to create a memorable rhythm in your presentation.

Repeat key phrases or ideas to emphasize their importance to your audience. During the OJ Simpson trial, when Attorney Johnny Cochran referenced the glove that purportedly didn't fit OJ's hand, he routinely made the statement, *"If it doesn't fit, you must acquit."*

Using repetition reinforces the message and assists your audience in remembering it. This can be particularly effective when delivering complex or technical information. Repetition can also be an effective way to create a theme in your presentation that ties everything together.

Start by choosing a key phrase or idea that captures the essence of your message. This could be a quote, a metaphor, a statistic, or any other memorable phrase that resonates with your audience. Incorporate interactive elements into your presentation that allow your audience to participate in a playful way.

I have a colleague who uses a distinctive southern accent when delivering important points in his speeches. After making these key points, he reinforces them by encouraging the audience to respond with a unique southern phrase, "you bet!" This signature phrase becomes a recurring feature in his presentations, effectively reinforcing crucial concepts in the minds of the audience.

Once you've chosen your key phrase, use it throughout your speech to reinforce your message and create a theme. You can repeat the phrase at the beginning and end of your speech, or use it as a refrain throughout your presentation. Vary your delivery of the key phrase. Change the tone, pace, or volume of your voice. Use different inflections or gestures. Keep your audience engaged!

Repetition can be a powerful tool when used effectively in public speaking. When introducing key concepts or ideas, use repetition to create a memorable rhythm in your presentation.

Chapter 13

Sustaining the Improv Mindset for Success

The "improv mindset" is a way of thinking and approaching challenges that is grounded in the principles of improvisation. In the context of business, the improv mindset involves being open, adaptable, and collaborative in the face of uncertainty and change.

Implementation

Improv skills, like any other skill, require regular practice to maintain and improve. Consider taking improv classes in your area to continue honing your skills. There are many improv classes available in-person or online. At *The Outcasters*, we hold weekly online classes as well as live classes in Scottsdale, Arizona. Visit us at www.TheOutcasters.com. Also, attend improv shows whenever possible to see the principles in action!

As a leader, model improv techniques in your own work. To empower your staff to sustain the improv mindset for long-term success, reinforce its importance in communication. Remind them of the benefits of using it in their work. Explain how it can assist them in achieving their goals, as well as how it can benefit the organization as a whole. Offer regular opportunities for your staff to practice improv principles. This could include regular team-building exercises, brainstorming sessions, and other collaborative activities that encourage active listening, "Yes, and..." thinking, and risk-taking.

CEOs Embracing Improv Training

Join the many company CEOs who embrace the principles of improv in their day-to-day operations:

Satya Nadella, CEO of **Microsoft**, has emphasized the importance of empathy, listening, and collaboration in his leadership style, which aligns with many of the principles of improv.

Tony Hsieh, former CEO of **Zappos**, is a proponent of the "Yes, and..." approach to leadership, which he believed fostered creativity and collaboration within his organization.

Bob Iger, former CEO of **Disney**, has spoken about the importance of risk-taking, adaptability, and flexibility in leadership, which are key principles of improv.

Eric Ryan, co-founder of **Method and Olly**, has used improv principles to drive innovation and creativity within his organizations, encouraging his staff to take risks and try new things.

Ben Horowitz, co-founder of **Andreessen Horowitz**, has emphasized the importance of vulnerability and authenticity in leadership, which are key tenets of improv.

Jeff Weiner, CEO of **LinkedIn**, is a strong advocate for using improv principles in business. He believes that improv can help businesses to be more creative, innovative, and agile. Weiner has implemented improv training at LinkedIn, and he has seen firsthand the benefits that it has brought to the company.

Elon Musk, CEO of **Tesla**, and **SpaceX**, is a passionate advocate for the use of improv in business. He has said that improv is "one of the most important skills you can have in life." Musk has implemented improv training in his companies, and he has seen firsthand the benefits it has brought to the companies.

So... why not add your company to the list of progressive organizations harnessing the effectiveness of improv in business communication?

You cannot be guided
unless you're moving.

— Joe Hammer

Chapter 14

Take-Aways of Improv in Business Communications

Improv skills are a valuable asset for anyone looking to enhance their communication skills and excel in the business world. You will improve your ability to think on your feet, communicate effectively, and work collaboratively with others. These skills will not only improve your business communications, but they will also contribute to your overall personal and professional growth.

Let's take a look at the "Take-Aways" from developing powerful, life-changing improv skills:

Take-Away #1: Improved Communication Skills

Improv skills are invaluable in business communications, allowing you to become more confident, agile, and adaptable in your interactions with colleagues, prospects and clients. Improv teaches you how to listen actively, which is essential for effective communication. When you're actively listening, you're not just waiting for your turn to talk. You're paying attention to what the other person is saying, and you're trying to understand their point of view. You're also asking questions to clarify anything you don't understand. You will become a better listener, collaborator, and problem-solver, and foster a more positive and productive workplace culture.

Take-Away #2: Stronger Relationships

Bringing improv skills into your business communications will help you build stronger relationships with colleagues, prospects and clients, driving better results. Whether you're negotiating a deal, presenting to a group, or simply engaging in casual conversation, the ability to think on your feet, listen actively, and build on others' ideas can make all the difference.

Take-Away #3: Increased Creativity

Improv skills will allow you to become more adaptable, creative, and effective in your communications. It helps you come up with new and innovative ideas. When you're improvising, you're not limited by your past experiences or knowledge. You're free to explore new possibilities and to come up with creative solutions to problems! You will embrace the core principles of collaboration, active listening, and risk-taking, enhancing your professional development to achieve greater success in your career.

Take-Away #4: Trust and Collaboration

Incorporating improv skills into your business communications is a powerful way to build trust and foster collaboration.

Whether you're a CEO, business owner, team leader or a frontline employee, the ability to improvise, listen actively, and build on others' ideas can help you navigate the challenges of the modern business world and thrive in a rapidly changing environment. You will discover that improv is also a great way to relieve stress and have fun. When you're improvising, you're not worrying about making mistakes!

Take-Away #5: Enhanced Problem-Solving Skills

In today's fast-paced business environment, the ability to improvise and adapt is more important than ever. When you're improvising, you're constantly faced with new challenges. You have to be able to think quickly and come up with solutions that you may not have thought of before. By bringing improv skills into your business communications, you can become a more effective communicator – all while building stronger relationships.

Take-Away #6: Improved Teamwork

Incorporating improv skills is an exciting and engaging way to build camaraderie among your team members. It helps people work together more effectively and build trust. When we're improvising, we have to rely on our teammates. We have to trust that they'll support us and that they'll help us succeed. By engaging your group with improv exercises and games, you will promote collaboration, build trust, and enhance the overall workplace culture. Improv techniques will help you and your colleagues communicate more effectively, all while enjoying the process of learning and growing together!

Take-Away #7: Transformation

Bringing improv skills into your business communications will be a transformative experience, allowing everyone to communicate more effectively, build stronger relationships, and achieve better results. Your team will embrace the "fail fast, fail forward" mentality, understanding that mistakes are a natural part of the creative process and viewed as an opportunity to learn and grow!

> When you're improvising, you're not limited by your past experiences or knowledge. You're free to explore new possibilities and to come up with creative solutions to problems!

BONUS!

Some Great Improv Exercises to Engage Your Team!

Improv is a powerful tool for improving team communication skills because it focuses on the core principles of effective communication - active listening, collaboration, and being present in the moment.

Like a professional athlete, "warm-ups" are always necessary before training, game or event. This helps avoid injuries and prepares the athlete for the process. The same applies to our brains. We can't just jump into business without taking some time to stretch our creativity muscles! Let's incorporate some "warm-up" improv techniques prior to launching your team into the meeting agenda...

To initiate these warm-up exercises, gather your team in a circle formation. In this setup, each team member stands facing someone across from them within the circle. This arrangement sets the stage for the exercises to follow.

Descriptor Me

One at a time, have each team member say their name, beginning with a "descriptor" word that begins with the same letter as their first name.

For example, *"Exuberant Ed," "Persuasive Paula," "Jittery Joe," "Mischievous Mike,"* etc. They each should also include an interesting gesture or body movement while saying their descriptor and name.

After each one does so, the entire circle then repeats the individual's descriptor, first name and gesture. This exercise not only helps everyone get comfortable with each other, but will also loosen up any nervousness in preparation for further dialog.

 # I Heard You Say...

As you've learned, a key skill in improv is active listening, or being fully present and truly engaged in the moment. To practice this, team members will participate in a role-playing exercise where they take turns speaking and listening to each other. This is done with a warm-up called, *I Heard You Say.*

Team members remain in the warm-up circle. One team member in the circle begins the exercise by making a simple statement, such as:

"I got a new puppy"

The next person in the circle responds by saying, *"I heard you say…"* and then repeats the initial statement. They then add more information or a related comment. For example,

"I heard you say you got a new puppy; crate training is a great way to teach puppies."

The following team member follows the same pattern, building upon the previous person's statement:

"I heard you say crate training is a great way to teach puppies. I'm not familiar with it, but I look forward to researching it."

This process continues with each team member in the circle taking their turn.

"I heard you say you're not familiar with it, but you're looking forward to researching it, I think the local humane society has information about crate training on their web site."

Note: Everyone must stay "on topic" and not stray from the subject matter. Further, there can be no "but" or negative statements.

Zip, Zap, Zop!

Zip, Zap, Zop is a classic improv exercise that improves communication skills, reaction time, and focus.

The team members remain arranged in a circle, ensuring that everyone can clearly see and hear each other. The activity commences with the first person in the circle making eye contact and using a karate-chop motion to indicate another individual in the circle while uttering *"Zip!"*

The person they pointed to then directs their attention to another participant in the circle, replicating the karate-chop movement and saying, *"Zap!"* The person who receives the gesture then continues the sequence, making eye contact with yet another participant and stating *"Zop!"* This sequence of Zip, Zap, Zop carries on multiple times around the circle.

This warm-up exercise is designed to foster present-moment awareness and attentive engagement. As the game progresses, the speed and energy of the clapping and pointing increases, making it more challenging and engaging. It's worthwhile to note that there are no specific rules or objectives in Zip, Zap, Zop - it's simply a fun and engaging way to warm up your team and get them ready to communicate effectively.

Zip, Zap, Zop is an effective way to start any team meeting or brainstorming session. It helps to break down barriers, get everyone focused, and build camaraderie and teamwork.

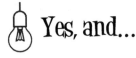 Yes, and...

The *Yes, and...* warm-up exercise is a valuable tool for reinforcing the *Rule of Agreement* in improv (see chapter 3). This exercise helps team members develop active listening, collaboration, and teamwork skills.

The team members maintain their circular arrangement. The process begins with the first member making a statement. The subsequent player in the circle responds using the phrase *"Yes, and..."* while contributing extra information that complements the ongoing conversation. This cycle carries on until all players in the circle have contributed dialogue. It's crucial to refrain from using "yes, but..." as it contradicts the principle of agreement.

For example:

Player #1: *I can't wait to go skydiving tomorrow!*

Player #2: *Yes, and... I'm sure your parachute will be safely packed!*

Player #3: *Yes, and... I trust my instructor to do a good job.*

Player #4: *Yes, and... if he doesn't, you won't have to worry about trying it again!*

Player #5: *Yes, and... I think I'll double check my insurance policy!*

Player #6: *Yes, and... be sure to include me as a beneficiary!*

While you can also use other affirmative connectors like *"Sure," "Okay,"* or *"Of course,"* it's recommended to start with *"Yes, and..."* until you become comfortable with the agreement process. This exercise helps solidify the concept of agreement and encourages a positive and collaborative mindset during improvisation.

You'll find it surprising how the story develops through the positive contributions from everyone in the dialogue!

 # Yes, Let's!...

The *Yes, Let's* exercise is a fun and collaborative warm-up improv game that encourages active listening and creativity.

The team members maintain their circular arrangement. This warm-up is started by someone in the group making a simple suggestion, such as

"Let's scratch our heads like we're confused."

While doing so, they also mimic the action. In this instance, the person is scratching their head while making a face depicting confusion.

Everyone else in the circle then responds with *"Yes, let's..."* and duplicates the physical action of scratching their heads and showing confusion.

The next person in the circle then demonstrates another action, *"Let's go fishing!"* while miming casting a fishing pole into the water.

Everyone else in the circle then responds with *"Yes, let's..."* and duplicates the physical action of casting a fishing pole into the water, and displaying a face of confidence as they're catching a fish.

The game continues until everyone in the circle has contributed their ideas. This exercise is a great way to encourage active listening, and creative thinking in a team setting.

 # One-Word Story

The *One Word Story* exercise is a fun and creative warm-up improv game that builds collaboration and storytelling skills.

With the team members remaining in a circle, the objective is to create a story, with each person taking turns adding only one word to the story.

The first person starts the story with a simple phrase, such as *"Once upon a time..."*

The next person in the circle responds by adding only one word that builds on the starting phrase, such as *"there."*

The next person in the group responds with one word that builds on the previous word, such as *"was."*

The game continues, with each person responding with one word that builds on the previous word in the story. As the story progresses, encourage your team members to use their creativity and imagination to create interesting characters, plot twists, and unexpected developments.

> **Player #1:** *Once upon a time..*
> **Player #2:** *there*
> **Player #3:** *was*
> **Player #4:** *a*

Player #5: *beautiful*

Player #6: *princess*

Player #7: *who*

Player #8: *worked*

Player #9: *for*

Player #10: *Microsoft...*

The process should persist until the story naturally concludes or until everyone has contributed multiple words. Steer clear of inserting words that don't fit the context of the story. For instance,

"Once upon a time, there was a beautiful princess who worked for Microsoft and smelled perfume..."

The phrase "smelled perfume" doesn't really connect with Microsoft—it's a mismatch that disrupts the flow of the story.

The One Word Story exercise is a great way to build collaboration skills and encourage creative thinking. It also helps to develop listening skills, as each person must pay close attention to the word previously said in order to add a relevant word to the story.

Pet Peeve Rant

Pet Peeve Rant is an improvisational warm-up that involves sharing a personal annoyance or frustration, and then performing a short rant based on it.

To play the game, participants share a personal pet peeve, such as people who chew with their mouth open, slow drivers in the fast lane, or people who don't wash their hands after using the restroom.

The person sharing their pet peeve should take it to beyond reasonable levels, adding bizarre reasons why it's problematic or even dangerous. Some examples:

"It really bothers me when people buy more than a reasonable amount of toilet paper at Costco. I can't help but think that their family must have digestive problems, excessively loose stools, IBS or simply consume too much fiber."

"Why is it that, when people buy bananas at the grocery store, they have to break off one or two bananas from the bunch? Are they that tight on money, or is their life so structured that they are only permitted one banana per day?"

Pet Peeve Rant is a fun and engaging way to get people to share their personal annoyances while promoting creativity and storytelling.

One-Word Expert

Similar to *One Word Story*, the *One Word Expert* game requires a team of 6-8 members. In this game, the team collectively becomes "one person." who is an expert in everything. They answer questions by adding only one word at a time. The objective is to create a coherent and sensible answer to audience (team members not participating in the expert game) questions.

Each team member takes turns adding only one word to the story, rotating through the members until they reach a logical ending. When they reach that point, they all look at each other and nod, indicating their success with a sense of accomplishment.

Question to the expert: *"Should I put pineapple on my pizza?"*

The first team members should start by somewhat repeating the gist of the question, one word at a time:

Player #1: *You*
Player #2: *should*
Player #3: *not*
Player #4: *put*
Player #5: *pineapple*
Player #6: *on*
Player #7: *your*
Player #8: *pizza*
Player #9: *because*

Now this is where the creativity kicks in...

Player #10: *it*
Player #11: *is*
Player #12: *against*
Player #13: *the*
Player #14: *Italian*
Player #15: *rules.*

Player #16, realizing the answer has reached a logical conclusion, looks to the other players and nods their head.

Occasionally, the answers may not make sense. This usually happens when a team member adds an unusual word that doesn't fit the story. There's no need to worry or get discouraged. Simply pose another question to "the expert" and give it another try!

Note: Small groups will require multiple passes, with players having additional turns in continuing the story.

Headlines

The team members maintain their circular arrangement. This warm-up is started by someone in the group making a simple suggestion of an unusual headline, such as

*"Local sheriff discovers three-legged alien at **Starbucks**."*

The next player in the circle then must use the last word in this headline for their own outlandish headline, such as,

*"**Starbucks** announces it will only serve ice lattes to people with freckles."*

The next player continues, again using the last word as their headline's first word,

*"**Freckles** are the latest cosmetic surgery fad – get yours today!"*

Continue until all players have an opportunity to craft their own wacky headline. This is an excellent warm-up game for listening and creativity.

Questions Only

In improv, we don't ask questions, but this game allows it! Gather 8-10 team members and form a line. Two members step forward and engage in a conversation, but there's a catch: *they can only speak in questions.*

Further, they cannot parrot back a question already asked. For example, a parroted response to *"Hey, would you like to go to the park?"* would be, *"Have you ever been to the park?"*

If one of them mistakenly makes a statement instead of a question, they are playfully booed by the other team members and go to the back of the line. The next team member then steps forward and continues the conversation using only questions. Continue with all team members in the same manner. This game is a fun way to embrace losing gracefully and find joy in the process!

Player #1: *Would you like to go to the dance with me tonight?*

Player #2: *What should I wear?*

Player #1: *Can you do the hokey-pokey?*

Player #2: *Have you ever put your left foot in?*

Player #1: *Are those your dancing shoes?*

Player #2: *What time do you have to be home?*

Continue the dialog as quickly as possible, keeping the dialog moving until one player makes a statement instead of a question.

Tip: Start your dialog with the one of the five W's, "Who," "What," "When," Where," Why."

The Alphabet Story

This game is a fun and challenging exercise that focuses on quick thinking, creativity, and word association. The goal is to create a cohesive scene or story by going through the alphabet and starting each line of dialogue with the next consecutive letter.

The first player begins their sentence with a word starting with the letter "A." The next player must respond and continue the conversation with their sentence beginning with a word, starting with the letter "B." This continues through all the players until the letter Z is reached.

Player #1: *Alright Tommy, here you go – the keys to your new car!*

Player #2: *Boy dad, I never thought I'd get a corvette for my first car.*

Player #3: *Compare that to the neighbor kid's junky Hyundai!*

Player #4: *Don't think I could ever be seen in THAT at my school...*

Player #5: *Everyone would probably laugh at you...*

Player #6: *Fat Billy, especially... he has a Porsche*

Player #7: *Glad you've been going to the gym Tommy;
I don't want a fat kid.*

Player #8: *Hug me, Dad; you're the best!*

This game challenges participants to think on their feet and actively listen. It encourages spontaneity, wordplay, and collaboration.

 # Verses

The team members maintain their circular arrangement. This warm-up involves the exchange of dialog among team members; however, it must be done *in verses*. The first player offers a simple statement, ending in a simple, one or two syllable word.

The next player must then provide a sentence, with the last word rhyming that that of their previous player. After this, they supply another line, ending with a different single syllable word, to which the next player must rhyme. The process continues with all players.

Player #1:
I think I'm going to my girl's house for a fine dinner **tonight!**

Player #2:
That's nice, and you should be careful not to get into a **fight!** *... Her kids may be joining you both for dinner as* **well**.

Player #3:

*I hope not, last time it wasn't all that **swell** ... They almost choked on her macaroni and **cheese**.*

Player #4:

*That never happens to me... I always swallow it with **ease**... I bet she's going to be excited to see **you**...*

Player #5:

*Yes she always does... like the morning grass embraces the sunrise **dew**... You should get a girlfriend; they'll make your life more **fun**...*

Player #6:

*I did, but after two weeks I was totally **done**.*

Tip: The best way to quickly arrive at a rhyming word is to recite the alphabet in your mind, placing each letter at the beginning of the rhymable sound. For example, if the word to be rhymed with is "will," go through the alphabet until one "works."

A̶i̶l̶l̶, Bill, C̶i̶l̶l̶, Dill, E̶i̶l̶l̶, Fill, Gill, Hill, I̶i̶l̶l̶, Jill, Kill, L̶i̶l̶l̶, Mill, etc.

Also, be sure to add a connector sentence/phrase before the rhyming element of the sentence, as shown in the example above.

Harness the power of these improv exercises to shatter barriers and foster a truly relaxed and open atmosphere within your team. These exercises are your key to breaking free from rigidity and embracing a more open, dynamic approach when initiating meetings or brainstorming sessions. Use them!

Alright my fellow adventurer, congratulations on reaching the exhilarating conclusion of our expedition through the thrilling realm of improv and its incredible potential to super-charge your organization's communication!

But hold on tight, because the journey is far from over. Reading this book is just the beginning; now it's time to ignite those principles and let them propel your organization to new heights. Don't just bask in the glory of newfound knowledge; you must unleash its power through action, and there's no better moment than this very instant.

We've all been there, holding a book in our hands, absorbing its wisdom, and feeling inspired. But remember, the real magic unfolds when we roll up our sleeves and put those insights into play. Are you ready to take the plunge? I can sense your enthusiasm bubbling up; it's time to make a commitment:

Are you ready to ignite the flames of innovation, embrace change, and turn these principles into a blazing force of transformation within your organization? The world is waiting for your greatness, so let's make it happen, NOW!

☐ Yes, Joe. I dig the strategies and commit to applying them!

Signed:

X _____

Date: _____

Kudos for Joe's Life Excel-eration Books...

"A delightful and insightful read, Joe Hammer has brought together the best teachings on "how the mind works," while adding his own creative genius. You will be energized and inspired! Highly recommend!"

"Joe Hammer gives significantly practical and easy to follow steps to approaching making changes in ones life through his innovative concept of the Unconscious Authority. The book is not only full of highly valuable resources and tools you can put into practice into your life today to make a positive change but is very enjoyable to read as well. Joe's approach addresses what many self-help/personal developments books fail to do, addressing the root causes of problem areas in our lives. Highly Recommended!"

"I love this book. It's a short, powerful and potentially life-changing read - written in a most engaging fashion. Buy it, read it and learn how to question what you believe about yourself and discover why you behave the way you do. Next, discover an effective way to unravel the nonsense you have historically accepted as fact about yourself, and then use the techniques in the book to become the person you need to become, to do the things you need to do, to get the things you want to have. Highly recommended."

"We are always looking for new ways to expand our services. The 'Unconscious Authority' has allowed us to break through old thought patterns and discover the proverbial light at the end of the tunnel. We not only have expanded our listener base, but also found opportunities that were dormant to us. Thanks for the great book Joe! "

"Joe's approach addresses what many self-help/personal developments books fail to do, addressing the root causes of problem areas in our lives. Highly Recommended!"

"It feels just amazing when one can take control of what couldn't be achieved before! Not only my life is changing but the ones around me are feeling that powerful change as well. Kids, family, co-workers and friends! I highly recommend this book to everyone!"

"It's a great approach for breaking through unconscious barriers in your life. I highly recommend this book!"

"A rather unusual 'self-help' book that presents techniques to just tweak or make over those issues that prevent success. Well written, with easy to understand facts and principles that can be applied right now."

About the Author

Joe Hammer is a nationally recognized corporate improv coach and business-development trainer, sharing invaluable improv communication strategies with forward-thinking companies nationwide. As the Director of *The Outcasters Improv Training Center* in Scottsdale, Arizona, he's dedicated to teaching the principles of improv.

With a rich history of conducting numerous seminars and workshops for progressive organizations of all sizes, Joe's training emphasizes co-creation, spontaneity, and clear communication. He helps his clients develop essential business and life skills, nurturing their creativity with encouragement and resilience.

Joe is also the author of *The Improv Edge—How the Art of Improv can boost your confidence, enrich your life, and fast-track you to a more energized and motivated presence!* and *The Unconscious Authority, How to break through your mind's barriers, unleash your dormant wisdom and banish limitations in your life, relationships or career.* Joe's passion for training shines through in his practical programs, making them engaging and enjoyable learning experiences.

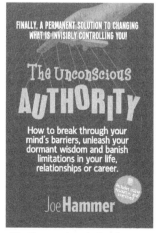

TheImprovEdgeBook.com   TheUnconsciousAuthority.com

For Joe's Small Business Development programs, please visit: ThatSmallBusinessGuy.com

For a wealth of student and client testimonials, please explore Joe's websites, YourImprovCoach.com and TheOutcasters.com

Bring Joe In...

Are you ready to break free from rigid thinking, enhance social skills, and bolster self-confidence among your staff? Your organization's training doesn't have to be such serious business!

Joe Hammer's **Influential Interactions** training – it's Serious Fun!

If you're in search of corporate training that seamlessly combines enjoyment with education, Joe's improvisation-based training is your ultimate choice. Joe's dynamic Influential Interactions training programs are designed to impart the essential principles of collaborative problem-solving, trust-building, and effective communication within your organization.

It's a Departure from Traditional Training...

In a world where change is the only constant, traditional training and leadership development programs are no longer as impactful as they once were. This is where Joe excels.

Joe crafts mindfulness-driven training programs tailored for organizations, specializing in key areas such as leadership, executive presence, public speaking, team building, and change management.

Joe's innovative techniques not only drive behavioral change but also rewire the brain to yield sustainable results. Through Joe's improv-based learning approach, individuals break free from established patterns, cultivate behavioral shifts, and tackle challenges with newfound perspectives. The outcomes encompass fresh skills and behaviors that offer immediate practicality in both personal and professional realms.

Rest assured, your organization will receive real-world, pragmatic solutions!

Contact Joe: Joe@YourImprovCoach.com | 480.612.0298